Me and My Cat

Me and My Cat

Carmel Reilly

Constable • London

Constable & Robinson Ltd
55-56 Russell Square
London WC1B 4HP

This edition published by Constable,
an imprint of Constable & Robinson Ltd 2012

A copy of the British Library Cataloguing in Publication Data
is available from the British Library

ISBN-13: 978-1-78033-482-0

Printed and bound in the European Union

1 3 5 7 9 10 8 6 4 2

Contents

Introduction   1

Funny Cat Tales   5

Emotional Cats   19

The Greediest Cats   49

When Cats Choose Their Owners   65

Cats with Attitude   81

Cats and Other Animals   105

Top Cats   117

Cats and Children   125

The Wandering Feline   133

Kitten Stories   141

Cats and their Nine Lives   159

Magical and Amazing Cats   169

Rescue Cats   183

All Kinds of Cats   207

Crazy about Cats   239

Introduction

I have a fond memory from my babyhood of being snuggled up to a warm fuzzy presence. It wasn't a teddy bear or any other cuddly toy. It was a cat called Tiger, the family cat which liked to snooze next to me in my pram but was only allowed to do so when my mother was there to supervise so that I would come to no harm. Tiger would purr loudly and send me to sleep, my mother said, and acted as a kind of guardian. I could feel Tiger's affection for me and I grew to love him and, through him, other cats.

During my life I have rarely been without the companionship of a cat and it is unthinkable that I would willingly choose otherwise. I am aware that there are many other people who feel the same way as I do. When I ponder why we cat lovers feel so attached to cats, I believe that it is due to the rare and special qualities that cats possess which beguile, charm and enchant us. In addition, for me, there is something indefinable inside me which has a feelgood effect whenever I am near a cat. It is not something I can fully articulate, it simply exists. It emerges as an attraction which I cannot resist, and perhaps it is so for the many other people who are slaves to cats.

My wife Catherine knows me better than anyone else but there is a part of me which can only be reached by a cat. When I meet cats that I haven't met before, they usually appear to recognise something in me to which they instantly relate with miaows, purrs and flicks of the tail. Their presence close to me, especially if we are old friends, makes me feel special and I begin talking to them as I would to a person. Cats are good listeners and to people who share their lives they show non-judgmental, unconditional acceptance of anything that is said. It does not matter to a cat how you look or are dressed. Cats, like other animals, judge a person by the feelings they express and by the ways in which they behave towards them.

Cats can also be very caring. They are quick to note distress in people and will often attempt to soothe the person simply by being close like a comfort blanket. Stroking a cat on your knee can have a therapeutic outcome. It will often make you feel better after you've had a bad day and usually restores calmness and ease to a stressed personality. But as all cat lovers know, you can only gain a cat's love if you are prepared to work at the relationship. A cat will respond to you solely on its own terms, that is if you take the time and effort to make friends with it. It does not give its love cheaply and will demand a degree of indulgence and worship from you first. When the cat is satisfied that you are a genuine friend and prepared to minister to its wants and comfort, then you will be treated to reciprocal love and adulation. It's a complex relationship in which a cat will sometimes deliberately ignore you because it has something of its own to think about: cat things which humans do not understand. It is the cat's superior air of independence, that autonomy of mind, which can be so irritating to us but which also endears us to them.

Human relations with cats go back a long way in history. The cats that first approached and joined human settlements were accepted initially for their services in killing vermin to protect food stores but their loving attributes were eventually recognised and they were adopted as pets. Their service to mankind is extraordinary and known throughout the world. When they join a household they bring companionship to the lonely and aged as well as joy to the younger generation, for who can resist the playfulness of a kitten? By the expression of their personalities they inspire people to prize them and want to extol them. We all tend to feel sentimental about our cats but it should be recognised that cats return the sentiments of love and affection we have for them with interest.

The number of books written about cats far exceeds that for any other animal and the amazing phenomenon is that men and women still go to extraordinary lengths to share the uniqueness of their beloved pet cats with friends and a reading public which has a huge appetite for cat books. It is surprising how lovingly we regard our cat friends. When a cat of mine dies my sorrow and pain at the loss knows no depths. It is akin to losing a beloved family member which is the role our cats fulfil for us. To pluck a quote from Shakespeare's Hamlet and apply it to our feline friends: "What a piece of work is a Cat."

As for me, I think my two Maine Coon Cats, Luis and Max, are not just wonderful but even more than this, as my wife and I could not contemplate life without them.

Denis O'Connor (author of *Paw Tracks in the Moonlight*)
October 2011

Funny Cat Tales

I've spent the last year gathering first-hand accounts from cat owners.
Among the many and varied responses I received, there were a lot of
humorous stories about the funny things that cats do, so I thought we
should start with a selection of these.

A Cat Bearing Gifts
Billy, 52

I used to have a Bengal cat called Bobo and he was just wonderful
at bringing in presents on a regular basis. I have been told that when
cats bring you presents they're supposed to be food offerings but I
think that the gifts brought to me by Bobo sometimes had other
motives.

Bobo was very possessive of me and hated it when I had other
people to stay. My mother-in-law was once presented with a filthy
old boot and a friend of my husband's who I really didn't like very
much was given a very smelly and rotting carrot, placed right next
to his pillow for when he woke up. I have been given dead birds and
rodents but the strangest present of all was a small tub of hyacinths,
dragged in through the cat flap and pulled upstairs to my bedroom.

It was still in its pot and had lovely sweet smelling blue flowers still planted in its soil. I've never known a cat to bring anything like that. I put them onto my bedroom window sill and watered them regularly and they were in flower a long time. During late summer I dug up the bulbs and put them in a bag in the airing cupboard so that I could plant them the following spring. Each time they come into bloom Bobo sits on my bed with me looking at them and purrs loudly.

Playful Tilly
Joan, 36

I have a cat called Tilly who is a busy, playful young tortoiseshell female. She loves to play with me. She seems to have worked out that I play with her more when she brings me something that I find amusing for her to play with. I could spend all day playing with her but I work from home in my office in the spare bedroom. I also have another cat called Ben who is an older male and who considers the upstairs to be his domain and will not tolerate Tilly being on the first floor.

One day I heard a furious caterwauling coming from downstairs. I looked down from the railings on the landing, and saw Tilly standing next to one of my sheepskin slippers that she had dragged out from the downstairs bedroom where I sleep. There were three shoes around her that she had apparently pulled out of my bedroom and it was clear that she wanted me to be downstairs and playing with her. As I went downstairs Tilly began purring as hard as she could and I didn't have the heart to refuse to play with her so we spent half an hour together in the hall. I can't do that every day and it appears that Tilly understands that. Sometimes I find her playing with my slippers at the foot of the stairs by herself but she is always happier if I go downstairs for a few minutes.

Banjo and Bella
Jackie, 33

Both my cats are little rascals. Banjo is a large brown Burmese male and rules the house. Bella is a tiny black female cat who is very sweet-natured but rather plump. Banjo is very cuddly but also very opinionated. Whatever you try to do, whether it is reading, sewing, cooking or trying to work from home, Banjo is right there in the middle of it all. You can tell when he's building up to a demand for complete attention.

Bella spends her days finding new ways to show us her tummy, inviting us to give it a rub. She's mastered the art of getting someone to pet her whenever she chooses. She loves to hide, thinking nobody can see her, whether it is in a box, beneath a rug, or under the coffee table. She's funny in a sweet, loving way, but you would have to love cats to really appreciate her distance and her humour.

Banjo is about a year younger than Bella, and he still remains the naughty kitten. He loves to jump and climb onto everything, from the refrigerator, to the windowsill, to the top of doors. He is an acrobat who can balance himself on the narrowest of ledges. There is nowhere in our home that he hasn't explored or sniffed, from the tops of bookcases to the cupboard under the bathroom sink.

As long as he stays off the kitchen work tops and dining room table, we pretty much let Banjo jump and climb anywhere he wants to. He's agile enough not to knock things over or scratch anything during his playtimes. There was one night however, when even Banjo surpassed himself. He had been outside having a sniff about when he jumped on top of our compost heap. My husband had recently filled it much higher and somehow Banjo got stuck in it. We heard a loud yowl and then some scrabbling noises. When we went into the garden there was Banjo up to his neck in compost. His paws had got covered in compost so he couldn't dig himself out.

My husband had to get a shovel to get him out. When he came back into the kitchen he smelled absolutely terrible. Bella took one sniff and, because she didn't recognise his smell, growled and ran off to hide. I had to take him upstairs to the shower and after his earlier trauma he took it very badly, I had to wrap him in a towel to wash him or I would have been scratched to bits.

Eventually, we got him clean and dry and Banjo doesn't go anywhere near the compost heap now.

Odd Habits
Sam, 40

I have a cat called Felix who jumps up and taps my back from behind. It's always quite startling because you don't know that he's about to do it. If I'm doing the dishes or preparing food he sneaks up behind me and launches himself at my back. He also stretches up my back legs while I am standing and paws at my thighs. I think it happens when he's feeling playful. I have to stop what I am doing and chase him, he loves it. Sometimes he just wants to play chase and sometimes he will run and then stretch out on the carpet to have his tummy tickled. He also knows that if he jumps in a cardboard box, he will get attention because I find it so funny.

A Cat in the Bath
Geraldine, 29

I have a cat called Tod who is obsessed with the bath. When I first brought him home he got straight into my bathtub and settled down to sleep. I offered him a blanket and a chair for a bed but no, he wanted to sleep in the bath. If anything ever scares him he goes straight to the bath and gets in it. At first I worried that he wouldn't like it when I actually had a bath but in fact, it was just the opposite. If I got into the bath, so did he, but he seemed to hate being wet and always jumped out again quickly.

He also likes to join me in the shower. He jumps in then jumps straight out again, soaking wet. Sometimes he gets all caught up in the shower curtain and falls back into the bath, sliding around as if he's on skis. I always end up gently picking him up out of the water.

This often goes on for a while; him jumping into the water, and me rescuing him. If he doesn't like water, why does he do it? When I get out of the bath he watches the water as it drains down the plug hole and swipes at it with his paw as if he wants to kill it.

Tod always puts his paws in his drinking water too. He wipes his paw round and round in the water then licks it. It's as if he loves it and hates it at the same time. He gets fascinated when I do the washing up and often walks around the sink staring into the bowl of water with big dilated pupils.

When I go into the bathroom he races after me, pushes his way through the door and starts meowing at me. He jumps onto the laundry basket and shouts in my face. Sometimes he gets into the bath and gives me a defiant look that seems to say. "What are you going to do about this then?" He really is very strange.

Recently, I have started running 'play baths' for Tod. I make them very shallow, just enough to cover his paws and after a while I pull the plug out so that he can chase the water down the drain. He seems to love that, possibly because he doesn't get too wet. He can march around in the water for a full half hour before getting bored of it. I've even seen him sit down in the water too, giving him a very wet tail. Sometimes he tries to drink the bath water but it makes him sneeze.

When I go to work, I leave him a large washing up bowl with some water in it in the bathroom so that he can entertain himself whilst I'm out. Every evening when I get home he rushes to greet me leaving little wet paw prints on the hallway floor. He really does seem more affectionate since I've made him a paddling pool. He spends most evenings curling up with me purring contentedly. Even if I need to work on something in the evening he sits on my desk beside my computer gazing lovingly at me.

Juju
Lisa, 19

My cat Juju has an odd habit. If she sees anyone crying, she attacks them. She will bite their toes and then, if they are still crying, she jumps up at their legs and starts clawing at them.

Juju's now two years old and started doing this about a year ago. My sister was crying in her room and when the cat went to see what was happening, she got her toes bitten. The other day I was crying and she did the same thing, except this time she made a weird angry noise at the same time.

Juju is a very odd little cat.

Marbles
Megan, 35

My cat Stacy collects marbles. There is a little boy living next door and he often plays marbles in his garden. When he's out there Stacy will jump onto the fence to watch and when his back is turned she quickly sprints into his garden, grabs a marble and races back home with it to put it behind the sofa. She then spends hours scrabbling about down there with it, swiping it out from under the sofa then chasing it back again.

She also tries to eat balloons after they have burst. She went wild after my daughter's fifth birthday party when the children burst some of the balloons at the end. Unfortunately, they are not digestible and tend to come out in the garden!

Under the Sofa
Nina, 23

My cat Molly is very playful. Sometimes when I'm chasing her she sticks her head under the sofa but leaves her back end sticking out. I think that she thinks that I can't see her. I gently touch her back with my hand and she makes a 'brruh' noise. If I try to do some sewing she constantly makes a grab for the thread. She even pats me with her paw when I'm washing my hair. If I get up to use the bathroom in the middle of the night she's always in my spot on the bed when I return as if to say "Do you dare to move me?" There's never a dull moment with Molly.

Maurice's Antics
John, 32

My cat Maurice loves climbing onto our balcony railings to try to catch birds. Sometimes, he hides behind flower pots on the balcony in the hope that the birds will actually land nearby so that he can catch them easily but they never do. It's probably because he's huge and ginger; very hard to miss. Mostly the birds give the balcony a wide berth.

The roof of our downstairs neighbour's kitchen is about ten foot below our balcony and it's not unusual for some of the birds to land there, especially as our neighbour often puts out scraps for the birds to eat. Sometimes Maurice sits with his head through the balcony railings flicking his tail and squeaking insults at the birds on the roof.

One day last spring Maurice had had enough of them and actually jumped over our balcony onto the roof below. As he did so the birds all scattered and flew away, leaving our big, fat, ginger cat alone on the rooftop. The problem was that the kitchen is on the edge of quite a steep slope and it would have been too far down for Maurice to get off the roof that way. He was also too overstuffed to jump back onto our balcony so he was stuck there. Eventually he began to yell for help.

I went downstairs and round the side of the building trying to persuade Maurice to jump into my arms. He just looked at me as if I was mad and stayed where he was. I had to get the ladder and try to reach him that way. I prayed that my neighbour was in because the ground is too steep there for the ladder to be stable without someone holding it.

I was in luck, Roy, my neighbour, came round the side of the building after hearing Maurice's pleas for help. We had a difficult time getting the ladder into a stable place and I began to climb up towards my cat. As I reached the rooftop he looked at me with contempt and sort of slid down the wall of the building to the ground leaving me and Roy looking like fools trying to get to an empty rooftop.

When we put the ladder away, Maurice was waiting placidly at the door to be let inside, looking at me as if all the drama was my fault.

Attention Seeker
Rachel, 25

My cat is insane but I put up with him because he is very affectionate. He's an Abyssinian sand-coloured cat with green eyes. I often think he was a Prince in his past life. He has a foot obsession, destroys sofas, chews doors and loves walking on the kitchen table to annoy me. He will do anything for attention. Human behaviour fascinates him and he always needs to be near me. He seems to get separation anxiety if I leave the house for a day.

The Bedroom Door
Joe, 36

My former cat Harley had an odd trick. He somehow figured out how to knock on my closed bedroom door. It wasn't pawing at the door but actual knocking. It sounded like someone was desperately trying to wake me up due to an emergency of some sort but when I opened the door all I'd find was a ginger cat looking expectant. The first time it happened I actually got mad at my flat-mate, assuming he was playing a joke on me.

Harley also used to crouch behind doors and leap out on your toes when you walked by. He was a loveable nuisance because he must have weighed about 15lbs and it hurt when he smacked into your foot with all his claws out. He lived to be about fifteen years old and died out in the garden one night.

I still miss that cat.

Mina the Rabbit
Dawn, 37

Let me tell you that Mina is my cat and she is one year old. I used to live in the country but I moved to the city some years ago. I moved to a large flat and I was given Mina by a neighbour. Mina was very small and shy when I first got her; she used to hide under the furniture.

Now however, she's the coolest cat, I think she doesn't consider herself to be a cat, instead of trotting the way that cats do, she jumps like a rabbit, and she's always chasing anything that moves. She also likes to play with her toys, at night she brings her toys to me and drops them on the floor in front of me. I have to throw them and she bounces off to catch them, and bring them back.

She can play that game for hours, long after I want to give up.

Close to You
Claire, 35

My cat's called Minky and her favourite spot is in her cat bed right beside the computer where I work.

She loves to be near me. A lot of the time she will sit right next to the keyboard as well, until I coax her to leave and go back to her bed. When she wants something she will walk across the front of the screen repeatedly until I give her what she wants. She sometimes disappears for the night but if she's in she has to sleep right up next to me.

She's very inquisitive and picks new toys every week; sometimes it is a cardboard box or a bit of wool or a conker. She's funny that way. I think it's because she's quite intelligent. She often changes where she sits during the day as well. At the moment it's by the front door where the sunlight from the window in my door leaves a warm patch on the parquet floor. I guess her choice of different spots to lounge in makes her life more interesting.

Suzy and Malley
Jane, 20

I have two cats and they're both a bit odd. Suzy gets very startled and bolts from the room when anyone makes any sudden movement. She's very easily frightened. She also loves chocolate cake and almost anything else that's sweet. I find this strange because someone once told me that cats can't actually taste anything sweet. I don't know if that's true or not but Suzy seems to enjoy it so she must taste something. I try not to give her too much though because I know sugar is bad for their teeth.

My other cat Malley hates the sound of an aerosol can. He goes crazy and runs away to hide. I think it's because it sounds like a cat hissing at him. Malley also gets really mean whenever Suzy is around. He's very jealous of her because she's quite attention seeking.

Malley will sneak up behind Suzy and, without warning, bite the backs of her back legs where they are most bony so it hurts. She always gives him a smack afterwards but he never takes any notice of that; it doesn't deter him. Both cats love to play with paper bags. One gets in and the other jumps on the cat in the bag. They also attack human hands in paper bags too, though I sometimes turn the tables and get my 'hand in the bag' to attack them. This freaks them both out!

Harry the Office Cat
Mark, 40

There is an office cat where I work called Harry. It's a family company and they are quite relaxed so it is not as unusual as it might sound. Harry always has to sit in my in-box even though he is about half a cat too fat for it. He also insists on sitting on any pieces of paper that are on my desk, no matter how many other places there are to sit, if there is one sheet of paper on the table, you can be sure he'll sit on it. It sometimes means that I'm not as productive as I might be but I love him being there. It somehow makes it seem less like work.

Miss Paws
Sarah, 46

My cat Miss Paws, loves those shiny-coloured foil chocolate and sweet wrappers. If she sees you unwrap a sweet she's immediately over by your chair meowing for the wrapper. She likes you to roll it into a ball and throw it. After she's played with it for a while she will carry it off to her stash behind the shoe rack in the hall. Whenever I clean I find a little pile of different-coloured foil balls.

Of course, Christmas is her absolute favourite time of year. It is at this time of year that Miss Paws can get visitors to eat sweets and throw the wrappers for her too. I always have to warn guests that if they decide to have a chocolate they will be expected to join in with her game. In fact, they won't have any choice!

Garlic and Worms
Caroline, 70

I used to have a cat called Florence who collected worms. It was a nightmare because I'm really frightened of them. She would bring them in and leave them in a little pile under the kitchen table. Florence would sit on the kitchen windowsill and watch the robins on the grass and then go outside and copy them by pulling up worms. She didn't eat them; she just loved to pull them out of the soil. She also talked to flies by giving a little chirrupy sound whenever they flew around her. She hated all flying things.

Florence also had a thing about garlic. She loved to eat raw garlic even if it was still in its skin. If anyone was cooking with garlic Florence demanded to be given a clove to chew on. She would meow for garlic until she got her way. She often smelled of garlic when she came to snuggle up to you. She also ate olives and capers. I've never had a cat since with such a bizarre taste in food.

Emotional Cats

In this section we find sensitive and temperamental cats, as well as pets that comfort their owners, or respond to their emotional moods.

Chatty and Understanding
Ruth, 41

My daughter has Asperger's Syndrome and struggles with emotional attachments, finding them hard to develop herself and hard to understand others' emotional reactions to her. Having heard that animals could be good for anyone on the autistic spectrum, we adopted a Siamese cat called Mimi to see if there was any truth behind the rumours.

Mimi bonded instantly with my daughter, talking to her and rolling against her, purring. My daughter seemed to become attached to her immediately. Mimi put up with being held, snuggled, being stuffed into the front of a jumper and being made to sleep on a cushion on the bed.

To my surprise my daughter involves the cat in long complicated conversations and Mimi sits with her as if she is listening. My daughter has learned empathy as well as learning to express affection in cat acceptable ways. She also loves drawing and painting and Mimi fancies herself as something of an art critic. When she likes a drawing she lets you know by sitting on it.

Bruno the Carer
Elizabeth, 34

I broke my leg last winter and when I came back from the hospital with my leg in a cast my Siamese cat Bruno immediately seemed to settle into the job of nursing me. He would jump up on my bed and snuggle against me even though the cast must have felt hard and uncomfortable for him. My husband who was home when I had the accident (I fell on some ice whilst I was carrying the shopping home), told me that Bruno began to walk around the house making a weird wailing noise as if he instinctively knew that something bad had happened. Apparently he began looking behind furniture and jumping up on all the window sills trying to see outside.

The whole time that the cast was on my leg, Bruno rarely left my side. When I had the cast removed Bruno seemed to be as happy about it as I was and rubbed around my legs purring. It's lovely to know that he's as fond of me as I am of him.

Mr. Tail
Colin, 44

Mr. Tail wasn't like other cats. Throughout his life he thought he was a kitten. He would sleep in the bed with my husband and me and suck on our ears to wake us up. He was very vocal, outgoing and friendly and everyone on our street knew Mr Tail and would shout a "hello" to him wherever they saw him. He had a very distinctive white and black pattern, a black tail and "hat" and a few blobs of black, but otherwise he was white. Every night when I came home from work, he would be waiting by the door meowing and turning round and round as I climbed the steps.

We would touch noses and then he would go inside with me. He loved to drink out of a cup. He never drank from a bowl. Mr Tail frequently brought home birds, squirrels, mice and the occasional frog. Not pleasant to deal with, but I'm told that they bring these to you as a gift and he made sure that they were always waiting out in the hall by my shoes.

Sadly, Mr Tail was hit by a car last year and died instantly. We miss him so much. Eventually we will get another cat but it's going to be hard to replace Mr Tail.

My Soul Mate
Jerry, 49

I work as a vet and over the years I've treated many cats and never particularly liked them. They were hard to read and easily stressed. However, my attitude towards them changed when I met Sooty. Sooty was a male black cat; very sleek and very proud. As soon as I looked at him, I fell in love immediately. A woman brought him in because she had found him abandoned at the end of her street in a cardboard box, she didn't know where else to take him. As soon as I saw him I knew he would be coming home with me.

Sooty and I were so in tune with each other that he knew when I was tired, and he would nuzzle me to tell me that it was time to go to bed. My sister came to stay with me for a while and said that Sooty sometimes just sat on my bed and watched me sleep. He always wanted to be in the same room as me and would follow me everywhere.

I had my appendix out and whilst I was at home recovering, Sooty would sit next to me patting my hand to look after me. When I gave him a stroke, he pushed my hand to my chest and put both of his front legs over it, as if to say, "Don't worry about me, I'm here for you".

He died in his sleep after being with me for twelve years. He was the best animal to enter my life and although I have other cats now, I think of him every day, and thank him for being my friend and companion and letting me love him back.

Cat Woman
Mary 75

There was a time when my neighbours used to call me the Cat Woman. I had twenty-five cats that I fed at my back door. Gradually however, they either died or moved on and now I only have one, a cute little grey and white one called Pebble. Pebble is always with me.

When my brother died, Pebble could tell how unhappy I was. He used to come into my bedroom in the morning and instead of fussing for food like he normally did, he would get into bed with me and snuggle up to me purring. It was a real comfort to feel his little warm body cuddling into my neck and I am very grateful that he is there when I wake up because no one else is.

Tabitha
Donna, 20

During my high school years, life was hell. I had severe problems in school that made me feel really down. I skipped school for many days at a time and stayed in my bedroom for hours, just lying on my bed. I didn't want to talk to my parents because I knew they would reprimand me. Basically, I'd really lost interest in life and in mankind. I felt so alone and useless.

One weekend, my cousin came to visit and brought me a two-month-old tabby kitten. As soon as I put it on my lap, it fell asleep. We had owned a cat before, but that one never slept on my lap. I called her Tabitha and we set about getting used to each other.

Within two weeks the two of us were inseparable. I loved it when Tabitha woke me up in the mornings by lying on my chest purring. The mornings that used to be my worst times became really happy. My cat, Tabitha, was really an angel who saved me. It helped me through the hardest times.

Then, around three years after Tabitha arrived in my house, my grandfather died. I had to travel to my dad's hometown for the funeral. I was only away for a few days, then I went back home. Back home, Tabitha was so overjoyed to see me that she bounced all around the room, over all the furniture, quite literally jumping for joy. I had no idea that cats pined for you in the same way that dogs do when you leave them to go on holiday. I found it really touching, the way this cat showed such affection for me. As I said I'd been really lonely at school and it was so nice to have a little furry friend. I don't really believe in miracles, but if God really exists, I think He sent me an angel just to help me through the hardest times and I still thank Him for sending Tabitha to me.

The Best Cat in the World
Anna, 10

I am ten years old and my cat is my best friend.

Mum and Dad got her for me from the animal shelter. When they handed her to me she just looked at me and I said hello and she gave me a little meow to say hello back.

I held her for a while and she fell asleep on my lap. She sleeps with me and doesn't seem to mind having to move all the time when I want to do something different. She follows me from room to room and runs to my bedroom whenever I go there. She pats me with her paw when she wants my attention and I am the only one that she allows to hold her.

She is white with a black mark above her left eye. She loves to play with her catnip mouse. When she catches it she rolls over and over on her back with her paws in the air. She makes me laugh and always knows when I don't feel well. She won't leave my side if I am sick. She is the best cat in the world.

Patch
Beryl, 57

When I was a little girl we owned a white cat with black splodges on her called Patch. She was a great companion and loved to sit on my lap when I read books. I spent many happy hours playing with her kittens and teaching them to jump over my hands on the floor. I noticed that if I was ill she would pay me even more attention than usual and she would stay with me purring intently as though she was willing me to get better. She died when I was fourteen and I missed her terribly.

That was over forty years ago and just recently a cat that looks very similar to her has started to appear in my garden. I've taken to feeding her in the hope that she will stay with me.

Lost Hearing
Helen, 64

My white oriental shorthair cat, Gillon, began making a strange wailing noise so, because something was clearly wrong, I took him to the vet. The vet did a full blood test on him because apparently a cat can behave that way when they have a bad illness. Fortunately, all the blood tests came back normal and the vet suggested that he might have become deaf. I didn't really think he could be, because he has seemed to be able to hear me his whole life.

The vet tried various tricks to ascertain if he had indeed lost his hearing. The most telling was when he shook a metal can filled with coins, behind Gillon's head directly between his ears. He said that cats hate that sound. A cat in a cage behind the vet shrunk to the back of it, but Gillon did nothing other than twitch his ears slightly. He could sense the vibration but couldn't hear the noise.

It's quite sad really. He no longer runs into the kitchen when I open a tin. His ears no longer twitch when I call his name and clapping loudly behind his head when he is up to something he shouldn't be gets no response.

I was told that the reason he has lost his hearing is age. I didn't think that happened with cats but it apparently does. He's nearly seventeen years old. He is a purebred oriental shorthair, and they are bred to a certain standard so it is nothing to do with the fact that white cats can have hearing problems.

I comfort myself with the thought that, for most of his life, he could hear my voice. He would purr when I whispered in his ear. He could hear and respond when I said "Gillon." He loved to make noises at the birds he saw outside the window. He always had the most expressive, twitching ears. Now, his ears stay front and centre, they don't move in the same way any more.

I still cuddle and whisper to him though and he still purrs when I stroke and talk to him. If he can't see me he gets anxious and starts to make his weird wailing noise and I have to go and stand in front of him so that he knows that I am there. I tell him that I'll always be there.

Cuddly Simon
Kath, 30

I think that I must have the world's most cuddly cat. He's two years old and he's called Simon.

Simon waits by my door every morning for me to wake up, and then he follows me through the house to the bathroom. He jumps up on the counter to watch me whilst I brush my hair and teeth and put on my makeup. Weirdly enough, when I sit on the toilet he has to sit on my lap; otherwise he sits in front of me meowing. He has to lie in my lap when I'm sitting down or lie on my chest if I'm lying down.

If I even think of reading a book and not paying enough attention to him, he'll come right over and lie on my book, forcing me to interact with him. If I get my camera phone out to take pictures of him he knows it, and he gets all vain about it, rolling around the floor, and rubbing his face on the camera. Taking pictures makes him purr with pride because he clearly knows what a gorgeous model he is.

His favourite treat is tinned tuna and he'll do anything to get his paws on some. The only downside is how much he sulks if I go out for the day; and God help me if I go on holiday. That can lead to him sulking for a whole month.

Chatty Sasha
Katie, 16

We actually have four cats but I am the closest to Sasha. She follows me everywhere and she is very talkative. She always knows when I'm upset. She sleeps with me and when I wake up I say, "good morning Sasha" and she looks at me and meows. When she wants something she taps my arm or hand with her paw until I pay attention and give her what she wants.

She is quite a chubby cat because she loves her food so much and she always lies on her back to have her tummy tickled. I brush her and run a flea comb through her every so often and she loves it. When I'm upset she rubs against my legs or if I'm sitting down she'll get onto my lap and purr.

I love her so much.

My Cat is My Ears
Bel, 44

I have a wonderful cat named Blazer. I'm partially deaf and she's been such a good companion to me. She lets me know when the phone is ringing by running to the phone and she wraps herself around my legs when someone knocks on the door. She wakes me up when it gets daylight or just before the alarm is about to go off. She doesn't meow at the top of her voice so it's hard for me to hear her and she knows I'm hard of hearing. One day my daughter moved her washer and dryer into my laundry room. We started doing some laundry; Blazer didn't like the noise that the washing machine made and she suddenly jumped on me and pawed at me before getting off my lap and looking at me as if to tell me that I had to follow her. The laundry room floor was full of soapy water because my washing machine was leaking. I couldn't turn it off, so I turned the electricity off at the fuse box on the wall. It was lucky she made such a fuss about it. When the washing machine repair man came he told me that the water could have short circuited the whole house and might even have caused a fire.

The Kittens
Martina, 39

A few years ago, I let one of my cats have kittens. I gave one of the kittens, a fun-loving, feisty one, to one of my neighbours. However, the neighbour treated her badly and eventually I got the cat back.

Even though the neighbour was supposed to be caring for her, little Missy, as she was called, would come round to my back door every day looking hungry and so I would feed her. I mentioned this to the neighbour one day and he told me that he often had to go away on business for a few days and he just put a big bowl of food on the floor and left her to it. I decided that I may as well let her back in. She was still close to her mother anyway.

Both Missy and her mum My are indoor and outdoor cats. I have a cat door for them so that they can be independent. My is very special to me; I've now had her for ten years and there's never a dull day. I love her so much; she is quite maternal towards me. If I'm sick she comes and checks on me every hour and sleeps by me. She watches TV with me on the sofa. She really loves being with people. With My's daughter back in the house, the level of fun and games increased and I've had to issue a lot of telling-offs but they've also been a lot of fun. Missy is the naughtiest but that's probably because she is still quite young compared to My.

Three Cats
Andy, 33

I grew up with a cat called Benny and the loss of him was so heartbreaking that I didn't get one again for a long time. Shortly after we married, my wife really wanted to get a cat and I tried to talk her out of it for fear of getting attached to another pet.

Clearly that didn't work as we are now a three-cat family with two kids as well. Annie was the first, bought as an anniversary gift to ourselves. She is a feisty tortoiseshell Siamese who immediately decided that she was queen of the house.

She really hates the vet and can be temperamental but also very loving as long as it's on her own terms. About five years later, after having two children, we got another cat, a tabby female called Nora. I love her the most, probably because she loves being with the children so she keeps them occupied. She hates being picked up and the kids know not to try that but she likes her head being rubbed. She is obsessed with treats and has the loudest meow if you produce anything she deems tasty. You can't drink a glass of milk around her or eat anything without her sitting in front of you like a begging Labrador.

The third cat is a black shorthair called Jack. He wasn't even supposed to be our cat. About a year ago I was helping my mum get another cat from the rescue centre and my wife picked up this little boy kitten and demanded that we keep him. He puts his paws around your neck every time you pick him up and nuzzles into your shoulder. When he sits with you it has to be on your shoulder and it takes him forever to settle down. The two females are much more distant and independent than Jack, whereas he seems really happy being a very interactive pet and would always rather be with people than outside or with other cats.

I suppose eventually I will have to deal with these cats getting old, but in the meantime I have remembered how much joy they bring into your life.

Jonty
Gail, 39

I had my cat Jonty almost his entire life, from when he was about five weeks old. A friend gave him to me after his mother, a feral female cat, had been run over and killed. Jonty was found wandering around my friend's garden mewling for help. I agreed to take him in and hand rear him.

From the beginning Jonty was my special cat. When I went to work he followed me to the front door and then doubled back to watch me drive away from the living room window. He did the same thing in reverse when I got home again; waiting at the window then running into the hall. Apart from me, he didn't seem to want anything to do with other humans and viewed them with extreme suspicion.

I remember that one year he appeared to have found himself a girlfriend, (although I had already had him neutered). The female cat hung around the garden for a few weeks and even left him a dead bird on the patio table. For those weeks he trotted about with his chest puffed up very pleased with himself.

He was also a sensitive cat. He seemed to know when I was feeling down or ill and would always come to me to cheer me up (he even did this just days before he died). Sometimes he'd show me affection by biting my arm then snuggling up to me.

About two years ago, he began to have problems with his teeth and the vet eventually diagnosed FIV. It made it painful for him to eat and resulted in dramatic weight loss. He gradually lost the ability to groom himself and in the end began to suffer from kidney failure. The vet advised me to have him put to sleep and I reluctantly agreed. I still miss him terribly, especially when I see all the places that he used to sit in and remember his antics around the house.

Different Personalities
Jenny, 31

We have three cats, Peter, Paul and Joey. All of them have very different personalities.

Joey loves to do somersaults. He goes out into the garden and actually does a front flip, head over paws. I should video him doing them. Our neighbour thinks it is incredibly funny and brings her grandchildren out to watch him. He also has a favourite tin that used to have marbles in it. He can often be found asleep with his head on it. It doesn't look remotely comfortable but he seems happy with it.

Peter is a very talkative cat. He says hello every time you pass him. At first we thought it was his way of letting us know that he was around but I think he just loves to talk. If you speak to him, he will always give you a meow back.

Paul is a very tactile cat. He loves to sit on your lap. Every morning after he's eaten his breakfast he will climb up and sit on you. He is always making some kind of physical contact with you. He likes to reach out with his paw and touch you on your arm. Paul's actually my favourite because he's so cuddly.

No Boys Allowed
Helen, 27

I used to live in a small studio apartment on my own and my cat Freddy was very laidback. However, since I moved into my current house with some friends, I have noticed changes in him; he has become very fierce. I gave him a chicken bone the other night, and he ran off growling at anyone who came anywhere near him. So, moving into this house has brought out his tougher, territorial side. This has even extended to my bed. It's like living with my parents again, no boys allowed.

We also have a little kitten, Jims, who Freddy seems to have adopted. He almost behaves like mummy cat. During the day Freddy is more than happy to share my bed with Jims. It's not an uncommon sight to walk into my room, and see the two of them curled up together fast asleep. However, it's a completely different story when I go to bed. Then, Freddy gets grumpy and aggressive when Jims is in my room. I have to carry Jims downstairs and into the sitting room. After that, Freddy is suddenly a happy and cuddly cat again because he wants me all to himself.

Sally
Debbie, 42

We have a twelve-year-old cat called Sally who is diabetic. Early one morning last month she began acting strangely. She was walking around making weird noises and within an hour she was lying on the floor seeming very lethargic. She seemed unable to use her back legs and then she vomited.

Her breathing became shallow and I was very, very worried about her. I called our vet and told him that it was an emergency and the receptionist fitted her in immediately. We wrapped Sally in an old soft towel and rushed her to the vet's surgery in her cat box. In my heart I really thought we were going to lose her before we got there. When we were in the car, Sally's breathing became very erratic and once or twice I though she'd breathed her last breath.

The vet rushed her into the examining room and took her blood sugar level; it was at a dangerous level. We do get her tested often because of her diabetes and for a few months it'd been going quite well, but now she was pretty sick. However, the good news was that we had got her there in time. The vet got her blood sugar level back under control and also told us that she was developing arthritis in her hind quarters, which explained why she sometimes limps and seems unsteady on her legs.

When we got home, apart from the green bandage on her leg where they had taken a blood sample, she seemed absolutely fine. I am prepared to nurse her if her arthritis worsens because I've had Sally so long now and she has been such a good companion that I feel it's the least I can do to repay her for her affection. She seems like her old self again now and she's definitely glad to be home.

Tia's Concern
Maria, 58

Whenever I'm upset, nervous or sick my little cat Tia will start watching me with a look of concern on her face. Then she'll jump into my lap and won't go away till I'm smiling again.

I'm Not A Cat Person But...
Steven, 34

I don't have a cat but my girlfriend does. I have sort of adopted him because my girlfriend has moved into my flat. Now he's our cat and I call myself his daddy. He's a black cat and his name is Milo.

I wasn't really a cat person before I met him, but I definitely am now. He's a really calm cat and loves affection. Sometimes he'll get wired up and dash around the flat, but most of the time he's really laid back. One of my favourite things that he does is give me and my girlfriend massages. Yes, our cat is a masseur. If I lie down, he'll come up to me and rub me with his front paws. He usually likes to rub my stomach, probably because it's one of the softer parts of my body and he thinks I'm like a big cushion. Also, if I'm in bed and my girlfriend is across the room at the computer, Milo will climb onto the bed with me and curl up in her space in the bed. He likes to keep me company and be my cuddly toy when my girlfriend is out. I think it's because I started to feed him when I got up in the mornings.

Captain
Tom, 34

Some years ago I began a new job in New York and moved into an apartment with a friend. My friend had a huge Maine Coon cat called Captain. He was astonishingly large, I mean really, really huge. He must have weighed at least 20lbs and he had a really fluffy mane of fur around his neck. He stood in the hallway checking me out and then growled and sauntered off. To be honest I was quite intimidated by him at first.

Then, after I'd been there for about six weeks, I realised that he was in fact, a real softy. He loved to lie across my feet in the morning and share my breakfast at weekends. He didn't seem to know how big and scary he seemed to people. We would have friends over and they would be walking as close to the walls as they could, trying to avoid him. Captain for his part, would give a small growl then run away from them. I think he was actually a bit scared of strangers, and that only made him seem scarier.

Once he loved you though, he was like a big fluffy ball that insisted on sleeping on top of you, or sitting down in the middle of whatever work or book you had in front of you. There was one day when I was trying to write up some notes and eating a tuna mayonnaise sandwich at the same time. Captain loved tuna mayonnaise. I don't know how he recognised the noise, but as soon as he could hear you getting out the tin opener he appeared in the kitchen ready to lick the bowl out.

On this particular day, I was writing up a very important presentation that I was due to give on Monday as part of a bid for a large advertising campaign that the company I worked for was trying to win. I sat with my laptop on the table and was eating my sandwich when Captain arrived. He must have finished licking the bowl and he clearly thought that it wasn't enough and jumped onto my laptop trying to get at my sandwich. As he did so my coffee cup fell sideways across the computer and as I reached out to grab it I dropped my tuna mayo all over the keyboard on top of the coffee. The screen went black and then the computer died. No matter what I did it wouldn't switch back on. I really thought that the work that I had done all morning had been lost. I shouted furiously at Captain and he went and got into the cupboard under the sink in a panic.

I knew that the man who lived across the hall worked with computers so, praying that he'd be in I went and knocked on his door. He said that he could probably salvage the document I'd been working on but the computer was probably useless. I was extremely relieved when, later that day he came and knocked on my door with a CD Rom in his hand. I borrowed my flat-mate's computer and thankfully the whole document was intact. I was so relieved that at first, I didn't notice that Captain was missing but then suddenly missed him and went to look for him.

I found him still in the cupboard under the sink sitting all hunched up with his head down. It took me half an hour of coaxing to get him out. He was clearly upset that I'd shouted at him. That made me realise how sensitive cats are. Eventually he did come out for a cuddle and the best thing was that he never jumped onto the table when I was working ever again.

Nutmeg
Mary, 47

Nutmeg is like my child. I raised her by hand because her mother died after being hit by a car. She has always been the most precious and quirky cat. She enjoys nibbling on my ear as I am lying down trying to go to sleep, something she has done for years and probably will always do. I can't imagine life without my cat; she is my world, my life.

Lifelong Carer
Dee, 44

My part-Abyssinian cat, Tallulah, is ten years old now, but she is still looking after me. I have Crohn's disease and have been in hospital for numerous reasons over the years for surgery and some quite severe infections. Because I was tube-fed and confined to bed whilst in hospital I developed a blood clot, and then suffered with kidney stones. Tallulah is my little bed buddy, whenever I am recuperating from any sort of setback or illness. She seems to know when I'm not well and stays close to my side. I always look forward to seeing her when I get home from one of my hospital visits and Tallulah clearly perks up when she sees me. I have been told she sleeps more often and gets rather depressed when I'm not home to be with her. It is very rare that I leave her for a long period of time because I know what this does to her. My sister normally moves in to keep her company. Tallulah's a senior lady now and I want to spend as much time with her as I possibly can. She's given me so much comfort over the years that now she is old, I'd like to give her some back.

Milky
Annalise, 33

I have a Siamese cat called Milky. From being a kitten he has always been extrovert and friendly. He waits in the hall for when I come home from work and even sleeps under the duvet with me because he refused to sleep at the end of my bed the way that most cats do. If I don't let him sneak under the covers he tramples around my head trying to burrow his way in. He is a really faithful companion and loves to sit with me watching TV or sit on the kitchen floor watching me hopefully when I am cooking.

I have read that Siamese cats become very devoted to you and Milky is certainly no exception. He evens follows me up the road to my daughter's friend's house when I collect her from a play date there and waits patiently by their kitchen door until it is time for us all to go home. There is something truly special about Milky though, he responds to my emotions in a way that I've never known an animal to do.

A couple of years ago, I lost my grandmother several weeks after she had had a serious stroke. We had been very close all my life and even though she had lived to be ninety years old I was still very sad when she died. My mother had telephoned me to say that the doctor had told her my gran only had a few days to live. My family live a couple of hours' train journey from me, so I immediately booked a train ticket and travelled to the hospital where she was being cared for.

As I packed my bag I was feeling very upset and tearful and Milky just sat by me, occasionally putting his paw on my arm. Knowing that this was probably going to be the last time that I saw my grandmother alive eventually made me sit down and cry; Milky did the strangest thing. As I cried he looked me in the eye for a few moments and then began patting my face, where the tears were running down, with his paw. After each few pats he would then rub his head against my chest and then begin the patting of my tears again. He was actually giving me his version of a cuddle and a hug.

The fact that he could see that I was upset and then try to comfort me astonished me. It has made me love him even more. In the weeks following my grandmother's funeral there were often times when I began to feel upset again and he would always come to my side and look into my eyes in a completely different way than when he wants food or affection and play. One of those times he simply lay on the sofa next to me, lay his head across my chest and then stretched his front leg across me tightly like a hug.

He still follows me everywhere and shouts for his food like a screaming banshee but now I know that perhaps he is not just an entertaining pet for me to care for; he seems to care about me too.

Calm Benji
Maisie, 72

Through everything my cat Benji has been through (surgery when he swallowed a thumb tack, and now he's going to have to deal without me for a month because I have to go into hospital), he has been amazingly cool, calm and collective. He sleeps on my blanket or rug almost every single night and cries if I go on holiday. He truly misses me, which can't be said of some of the people in my life, so he's more than just a cat to me. He keeps my spirits up so he's very special.

Found in a Warehouse
Melanie, 30

My little cat was found by a friend of my husband, in a warehouse, when she was three months old. We took her in and she was so tiny and absolutely petrified of every thing. We bought her a cosy cat bed and some toys to chase and gave her plenty of food and love. She was very timid so we didn't fuss over her too much at first

She has slowly but surely started to come out of her shell. The vet says she will always be a small cat due to her first few weeks of life and she has a couple of odd little personality traits that we think are due to those first few months. As time has gone by, however, she has started to become quite a brazen little thing. At first she never purred, whenever I stroked her she would only allow it for a couple of seconds, and then lash out with her paw and move away from me. Now though, she's eleven months old and I've tickled her behind the ears, and stroked her gently until she eventually began to trust me.

Now, she will happily curl up on my lap and purr, purr, purr.

Cats Don't Like Me
Tony, 30

No one believes me but cats always attack me. I am always getting scratched by them, sometimes quite badly. It started when I was a little kid. I was stroking a little stray cat and it was being very friendly when it suddenly pounced on my head and began attacking me. I remember it screeching and hissing as I called to my mum to help.

As soon as she saw what was going on she came straight outside and chased the cat away. Even so, my head got clawed quite badly. It was really scary and I don't know if I give off some sort of scent of fear when I'm near a cat but since then all cats will scratch me if I get too close.

Stonk the Interactive Cat
Tim, 34

I got my cat, Stonk, from a newspaper advertisement. He was really sick and skinny and his current owners didn't want to keep him because they worked long hours.

I think he appreciates me taking him in and since he was a kitten I've been giving him a lot of love and every day I kiss him on the nose. Now when I get home he's always ready to come and lick my nose in return when I finally sit down with a cup of coffee. Stonk and I have a very special relationship. He talks to me all the time and I usually know what he wants; he has different meows for different things. If I say "food", he knows what the words mean and starts bugging me and running to and fro into the kitchen. When you say "go outside", he runs to the front door and waits to go outside with you into the garden. When I say "bedtime", he will follow me inside. Stonk also stays in his territory. He never runs off so I don't have to worry about him. He is very well behaved outside and he knows what "no" means. I've never had such an interactive cat before.

Calming Cats
Gina, 33

In my twenties I suffered from severe panic and anxiety attacks as well as depression. I was in therapy for months and took medication to try to stabilise my emotions. During this time I often felt very lonely as my depression made me reluctant to socialise. One day, I decided to adopt a kitten thinking that, maybe, I wouldn't feel so alone.

I got Sammy a week before my 26th birthday in 2003. I immediately felt I had a purpose, taking care of my kitten, and it gave me something to get up for in the morning. I enjoyed looking after Sammy so much that a couple of months later I adopted a little friend for him and added to our wonderful little family. Having them proved a wonderful distraction from my problems. So much so I feel I can handle my life a little better and I no longer have anxiety attacks.

I now have four cats and coming home to them is the best thing. I come home and I can talk to them and tell them my troubles and they patiently listen, (after they have been fed of course). My cats do seem genuinely attached to me and whatever room I am in they are sure to follow.

Daisy the Bad-Tempered Cat
Ella, 24

Several years ago I had a cat that I loved a lot. I had raised her from being a stray kitten. She kept coming to our back door and after a lot of begging, my parents let me keep her. She was half Burmese and because of that she could be a little dog-like but usually she was a sweetheart.

I called her Daisy because she slept in the daisies in the summertime. There was however, one problem; she hated my older brother's tabby cat Bess. There were always issues between the two cats, they would hiss and spit at each other and steal each other's favourite sleeping places but usually didn't actually hurt each other.

However, there was an incident about a year or so after my older brother had moved back home after college. Without warning Daisy attacked Bess and began biting her really viciously. I went to try to break them up and she turned on me. I got bitten over and over again and ended up with stitches in four bites on my arm. Afterwards, Daisy went back to being her sweet-natured self. I still can't work out why Daisy did what she did. I guess she was just jealous of Bess.

Boss
Lia, 44

In 1990, we adopted a cute eight week old kitten and called him Boss. He was black with a white bib and socks. He was very playful and grew up to be an intelligent cat who you took to immediately. He loved to have his chin scratched and at times would nuzzle your hand and put his head under it so you could tickle his ears. I have still never met a cat so clever. Every morning he woke me up just before the alarm clock was about to ring and he was always waiting by the front door to greet me when I got home from work.

I got divorced in 2001 and moved in with my mum. She suffers from asthma and I was able to teach Boss not to go into her bedroom or sit on her chair because it would make her wheeze. Even so, Boss loved to play with my mum when I was at work. He would come and sit in front of her and meow when he was hungry. She always knew when I was coming home because he left the house at exactly the same time every day and ran round from the kitchen to the front drive.

In 2005, I got a new job 200 miles from where we lived and we made the decision to move as a family (me, my mum and Boss), to a different part of the country. Boss was almost fifteen when we moved and he just seemed delighted with all the smells and new places to investigate. Every morning, after he ate, he would come into the study room, jump up on the table, and sit by the window while I had a coffee and read my e-mail. When I left for work, he would leave to explore.

In the evenings, Boss would lie down on my chest while I watched TV. When it was time to go to bed, I would turn off the TV and Boss would go upstairs and sit on his side of the bed. He even came with me to the supermarket, sitting on a blanket in the back seat. I used to get strange looks when I tried to find a parking space.

As he aged though, Boss became quieter and stopped going out to explore. The vet diagnosed a tumour in his kidney and said that nothing more could be done for him. We took him home knowing he wouldn't last long. We loved him, hugged him and kissed him and lay him down on the blanket that he liked to sleep on my bed.

He died that night aged nineteen years and I was heartbroken. I wrapped him in his blanket and we dug a grave in the garden by his favourite tree.

For such a tiny cat he shared so many of my ups and downs in life, I don't know if I will ever have a cat as close to me again. It is very hard to believe that he is no longer with me and going to bed alone still feels strange.

Go To Bed
Kayleigh, 25

One of my male cats, Founder, is my little angel. Every few weeks I have hospital treatment and as soon as I get home he makes sure I get to bed as soon as possible. If I am sitting up after it is over, he curls up, rubbing up against me and walking around me until I have a lie down. Sometimes, the side effects leave me in bed most of the weekend. Founder makes sure he is in bed with me, sometimes joined by his brother Roamer and his mother Flinky.

Emotional Stability
Chris, 43

I suffer from Asperger's Syndrome, which is a form of autism. It is very mild and most people wouldn't recognise anything wrong with me although they might find me a bit distant and cold. Since I have lived alone I have always had a cat. They seem to know when to snuggle up to me and when I need my space. In short, I find it difficult to comprehend my fellow humans, especially when they all seem to get caught up in each other's dramas. I feel very left out and uninvolved. If something is happening to someone else why should I react as if it's happening to me too? Anyway, emotionally, cats are far easier to cope with. I think we are closer to being on the same wavelength.

Clever Polly
Nina, 67

I have epilepsy and my cat Polly knows when they're going to happen. She isn't trained to do it but since I got her as a kitten she would come over and meow and paw and paw at me about thirty minutes before the seizure happened. It took me a while to work out what was going on. Her behaviour would be bizarre and then I would "zone out" as I call it. Eventually I realised that the two were linked.

I went to talk to my doctor and he said he believes that animals can sometimes pick up on these things. When my brain waves change, Polly starts butting my forehead and does not stop until I lie down. She sleeps on my pillow next to my left temporal lobe, as if that is the best way to keep an eye on me and when I am up and around she follows me everywhere. I am retired now but from my former job as an ADD specialist, I know first hand the uphill battle to have cats recognised as valid service animals. I believe that cats are very intuitive to their human owners' conditions.

A Box of Cuddles
Cal, 19

One night, the doorbell rang and when I went to answer it I found a friend of my mother's standing there with a box in her hands. Inside were two tiny tabby kittens that she told us she had found by the side of the road. She couldn't keep them as she had a big Labrador who wouldn't have been very impressed. They were so small that they couldn't have been much more than six weeks old and although we already had a cat we decided to adopt them. We called the boy kitten Diggles and the girl kitten Mandy.

They were both playful kittens right from the start. They loved chasing people around like dogs do, and they absolutely adored being picked up and cuddled. Diggles played the overprotective brother and always took care of his sister. It was really lovely to watch them. We had a bit of a scare when the kittens went missing one day, but it turned out that they were in a hole underneath the bathroom cupboard that the two of them had found and were enjoying being asleep undisturbed.

However, Mandy wasn't gaining much weight compared to her brother. She was still a little thing; she was playful but didn't seem to have much energy. I knew she was sick, and had to be taken to the vet. When she eventually stopped eating I knew it wasn't good. Mum wrapped her in a yellow towel and held her, trying to get her to eat or have something to drink, but it just didn't work. I stayed up extra late just holding her, petting her, and talking to her but she still seemed miserable. I put her and Diggles to bed on their blanket in the kitchen and closed the door.

The next morning we got ready to take Mandy to the vet but when we went to put her in the cat carry basket, we found that she had already passed away. Diggles was licking her face and seemed to understand that nothing could have been done for her. The vet said that she may have died from dehydration caused by an internal condition. We buried her in the back garden and Diggles looked on silently. I think we all felt very sad but even though she wasn't with us long, we gave her a lot of love and we still had her brother.

Diggles has always been healthy, thank goodness, and is a lovely playful cat. We will never forget his sister but I hope she is in heaven looking down and taking care of her brother in the way that he looked after her.

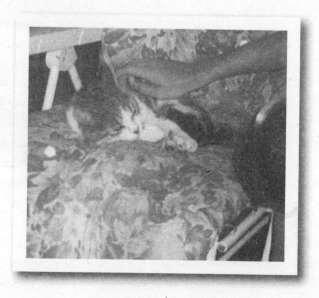

The Greediest Cats

Not all cats are greedy, but some cats do seem to be obsessed with food.
This section includes stories about gluttonous cats, cats who will stop at
nothing to find and steal food, or who demand constant treats.

Fat Sid
Eddie, 26

My cat Sid has always been extremely greedy. When he was a kitten
we used to have to lock up all the bread, cookies and other foods
because if we left them out on the kitchen work surfaces they would
get dragged onto the floor and partially devoured. We also had to be
fastidious about emptying the kitchen bin as things would be pulled
out of there too.

One afternoon I was working from home when I heard a ker-
fuffle breaking out in the kitchen. I had another cat besides Sid at
that time and I thought that perhaps they were fighting. I was
worried that they might break something so I hurried into the
kitchen to see what was going on.

When I got there, all I could see was a chubby ginger striped
back-end complete with legs and tail, sticking out of a yoghurt tub

as its owner ran frantically around the kitchen backwards, trying to get free. Sid had got his head stuck in a yoghurt tub, probably by pulling it out of the bin in a fit of greed to lick up any remains in the bottom of it.

By the time I got there he had got himself into such a state that if I tried to catch him to hold him still and remove the yoghurt tub, he began to fight with me too. Eventually I managed to get him into a position where I could take the yoghurt tub off his head and check that he was OK. Of course, there was absolutely no physical harm done to him but he glared at me the way cats often do when you've rescued them and they decide that their predicament has been your fault all along. After I'd fed him he promptly fled out of the back door. I think his pride was hurt more than anything else.

Many times since I've tempted him with a tub of yoghurt that has a small amount still in the bottom but it is possibly the only food that he resolutely refuses to eat, even when it is offered. He is still greedy about everything else though.

Chester's Trick
Luke, 32

I had a Siamese cat when I was little. Chester was an amazing cat, you could teach him to do tricks. If you held a little bit of biscuit for him, he would stand on his back legs and carefully take it in his mouth. He would also do this if I put a bit of biscuit in between my teeth with a bit sticking out – he would stand up and carefully take it from me. (My dad hated me doing that trick as he thought it was unhygienic).

He would also jump up so you could catch him – he would

stand at your feet, staring intently up at you until you patted your chest, then he would leap up, put his paws on your shoulder, and let you catch his back legs so you were holding him. There was a bit of a disaster one day when we had a visitor, a friend of my mum's. Chester was on the floor in front of him staring up at him. He had no idea that Chester wanted to do his trick so he just ignored him. Chester decided he was going to jump up anyway, so he made this huge leap. The poor man must have thought the cat was going for his throat as he let out a huge cry, and tripped over his own feet, falling backwards onto the stairs with Chester clinging on to his shoulder with all his claws. He ended up with some pretty painful scratches and a bruised backside. Chester ended up running off into the garden and hiding until the visitor had left – he obviously felt affronted that his cleverness hadn't been recognised!

Base Jumping Cat
Roy, 44

You know when teenagers do those tricks where they jump up and run along a wall or use it to jump up to a concrete walkway or whatever. Our cat Amber does exactly the same thing. She is a tabby, about three years old, and very lithe and strong. We have a garden shed which is about eight feet away from the top of the steps that lead up to the back door. The other cats can't even nearly jump onto it from the steps, but Amber has worked out a way of doing it. She leaps from the steps, twists sideways and takes a couple of big running strides along the wall, before twisting back round so she can land. Then she sits looking smug and waiting for the other cats to come by so she can torment them by sitting somewhere they can't get to.

I've seen her run down the stairs the same way once when she was startled, and she can also use the same trick in a slightly different way to get up onto the roof of the church hall behind our house – for that she runs vertically up the wall until she can cling to the guttering and drag herself up.

I've tried filming her as I would love to put my base jumping cat on the internet. However if you get a camera out she reacts as though it is a death ray and refuses to move until it has been put away, so thus far I haven't been able to catch her in the act.

Gina
Simon, 39

I have an eight-year-old grey tabby cat called Gina. I got her when she was three from an animal adoption centre. While all the other cats mewed and pawed at the bars of their cages, she just sat there with an 'I am a superior being' attitude. I knew immediately that she was the cat for me. She was the perfect single person's pet when I first got her; she loved to play and was very happy when I shared my food with her.

When my girlfriend Maria (who is now my wife) and I moved in together, things changed. Maria spoiled her. Gina started eating extra sachets of cat food and began lazing about as she got heavier. I would try to play with her but it usually just involved me waving bits of ribbon and string around while she watched with mild interest. Soon she began to look like a furry cushion. She ate constantly and food was so important to her that she felt compelled to wake us very early to start the first meal of the day.

Gina sits at the bottom of the stairs and howls every morning at sunrise. She's found that the most reverberant place in the house is our wooden floored hallway and so she uses it. She's also learned to stay just out of pillow range from the floor above. When she started doing that I thought she was hurt and hurried downstairs to see what had happened. She just walked casually to the cupboards where we store the food and waited expectantly. Maria and I have a deal where we take turns getting up, so that at least one of us gets a lie-in!

She's quite an old cat now and she's beginning to slim down. My wife and I have pledged not to get another cat for a long while after she's passed away, but I think we'll probably rebound to another pretty quickly. She's a spoiled, fat, loud cat but she's a great personality to have in the house.

Time for a Diet
Mark, 29

I have a super-fat cat called Tommy. He was so chubby as a kitten and as a young cat that when I first introduced him to a friend of mine, his remark was "Are you sure it's not a very pregnant female cat?"

Tommy began to get fatter after he was neutered. Now he's really huge. I keep the cat food on the breakfast bar to stop the dog eating it and Tommy can't even jump up there any more to steal it because he's too heavy.

He used to be terrible for stealing food which is probably why he ended up such a fat cat in the first place. A couple of days ago he sat on the floor chewing dog treats because he couldn't get onto the work surface to steal food.

He is a real sweetie though, very affectionate in his quiet way and he purrs at the drop of a hat. I've been thinking about taking him to the vet to see if I can get him on some kind of diet cat food, because he's so big and even though it looks cute, I don't want to lose him just yet and I worry that his weight will affect his health. I could do with losing a few pounds, so maybe we should go on a diet together!

Spike
Julia, 28

Our cat Spike is a very odd cat. He's a beautiful colour, a really deep orange or red colour with darker red stripes all over him. He loves to sleep with his head flat on the floor, making him look like a big furry slug. He also likes to get on top of items of furniture such as wardrobes, dressers and the fridge and jump on you as you pass by. When we first got him he was a scrawny little thing, all long legs and tail.

Now, he's a big chubby puss and must weigh about eighteen pounds. Sometimes, he sleeps on our bed and snores all night. He meows to be let in even though we have a cat door. I think he just likes me to run around after him.

Minky
Janice, 40

My cat Minky is a beautiful black oriental shorthair cat with the shiniest sleekest coat I've ever seen. He has large golden eyes and a very long tail that he likes to swish around when he walks. His legs are very long and his ears are enormous.

He likes to snooze most of the day and then comes to bed when I do and sleeps on my bed. I have twin boys and Minky loves going to their room and jumping from bed to bed without touching the floor. He can also jump from the dresser in my bedroom straight onto the bed (usually when I'm in it asleep and it's like someone throwing a football at you).

His other favourite pastime is eating. He is very, very greedy. Last month I was talking to my neighbour who told me that while I am out at work, Minky pops round to their house where she always has a treat waiting for him. She also said that he goes round to many other neighbours as well. He is well-known by the entire street. They know that he's not a starving stray but he is so handsome that they can't resist him.

I think that he's sometimes quite naughty though because the other day he came through the cat door with a piece of fried chicken in his mouth. It was still hot and the furtive way he rushed in made me think that he probably stole it.

Minky, like most oriental cats, is very attention seeking and has found a way to get onto our roof to chase off any birds that are up there. He gets up by climbing a large oak tree that is in our garden and then jumps from a branch that is close to the house. The magpies in particular jump around squawking at him to wind him up. They dive backwards and forwards around him and make a lot of noise but he seems to love it because he always goes back up there. He is good at catching mice and small birds but I think he'd love to get his paws on a magpie.

Genie
Jill, 39

My cat Genie has a tendency to walk around with her tongue hanging out. Another thing she does is to get into the coat cupboard in the hall and swing on the coats hanging there. If you happen to open the door while she's in there she'll leap out at you, which makes you jump if you're not expecting it. There's a scarf in the cupboard that she pulls down to make a nest out of. She's in that cupboard most evenings, we'll hear some rustling noises and we know exactly where she is. We once had a baby sitter who didn't know Genie's strange habits and was quite freaked out by her. She just heard noises coming from the hall cupboard and thought it was someone trying to break in.

When she enters the room, Genie always gives a loud meow to announce her arrival. She's so serious and determined when eating treats that she purrs as she eats and sounds like a goose. If you give her one of her favourite treat sticks she'll bite your fingers when she's finished it as if to point out that she's still hungry.

Porky
Gina, 24

Some years ago, we decided to have a barbeque on a lovely warm summer day. My dad set up the grill and put some big pork chops on it that had been marinated overnight. He even grilled some corn, pieces of chicken and spare ribs to enjoy later in the week because he knew how much both me and my brother loved barbequed food. The chicken, corn and ribs were done before the pork so my dad took them off the grill and took them into the kitchen, leaving just the pork chops to finish cooking.

Mum was in the kitchen making a salad and opening a bottle of wine, leaving me in the garden on my own. I had heard some meowing earlier in the week so I knew there was a new cat in the neighbourhood; he was probably investigating the area before laying claim to his territory. That day I saw a little tabby cat out of the corner of my eye. He was peeking out from some bushes. I pretended that I couldn't see him because I didn't want to frighten him away. The cat slowly started to creep out of the bush towards the little side table that was next to the grill. The next minute he was on the table looking with delight at the grilling pork chops.

I saw him reach out to one of the chops with his paw but I think the heat was too much for him. Still, he remained where he was clearly trying to work out how to get some food. My dad came out to turn the chops over but the cat stayed on his little table. I thought he might have jumped down and run away but instead it seemed like he'd invited himself to our barbeque. He wasn't scared of us. My dad said "Hello" to the cat and the cat meowed back. I knew that he must be hungry.

My dad turned the pork chops over and went back inside the house for the corn and salad and to get a glass of wine. When he came out he took the pork chops off the barbeque and began sorting them onto plates. I noticed that he'd brought out a small plastic plate too and he cut a little piece off each chop and put the plate down for the cat.

The cat was clearly starving and finished the food in about three seconds. He then stayed in our garden for the rest of the day. When we went inside later he sat on the back step meowing loudly. He obviously didn't have a home. After a lot of begging from me and my brother we were allowed to keep him. We called him Porky because of how we had all met.

Porky seemed to be able to take care of himself. My dad installed a cat door and he came and went as he pleased. He liked to watch TV with us and even followed the football if my dad was watching a match.

Sadly he died when I was about seventeen and I still miss him sometimes.

Potty Polly
Derek, 54

I used to have a cat called Polly who was famously a bit stupid. One day I was sitting at my kitchen table eating strawberry yoghurt when I heard a little meow come up from the floor. Polly loved yoghurt and often licked the remains from the tub after I had finished. She jumped onto the table in anticipation.

She put her paw into the yoghurt pot but instead of licking it off, she began to walk around the table. Then she sniffed the table where she had been walking as if looking for the yoghurt. She continued this, intermittently meowing at me as if to say "where's the yoghurt?" I pointed to her paw but as every cat owner knows, cats don't understand pointing. By this time I was laughing so much because she was getting more and more frustrated. In the end I caught hold of her and lifted her paw to her mouth. Only then did she get her yoghurt.

Cheesy Cat
Chris, 34

My cat Charlie really likes to be given cheese for snacks. When he came to live with me he quickly worked out where the cheese was kept and whenever I open the fridge door he appears, meowing for cheese. Sometimes he just comes up to me and gives me a meow that I know is a request for some cheese.

One day I was making myself some lunch and decided to give him a cheese treat. I called him but he didn't come. I turned to wash the knife in the sink and looked down to see where Charlie was. I couldn't see him so I called out to him and told him to come for his cheese. There was no answer and he was nowhere to be seen. I went to look for him but couldn't find him anywhere. Suddenly, I heard a noise in the kitchen and I went to see if he was in there and I hadn't noticed. I still couldn't see him.

Just then I heard the noise again. I turned around and listened and realised that there seemed to be something in my fridge clanking the bottles together on the shelves. I opened the door and saw Charlie. He wandered out of the fridge, looked up at me and meowed. I caught out of the corner of my eye the remains of the cheese in the fridge. He had pulled the plastic wrapper off the cheese and had begun to eat it. It was lucky that I found him quickly because he could have suffocated. I think he must have sneaked in when I got some milk to put in my tea.

Since then I always double check the fridge before I shut the door to make sure there aren't any cheese burglars around. I think he would be too big to fit in there anyway now.

A Cat Called Loopy
Billie, 27

I've been a cat lover all my life. I recently adopted a black cat who has a few small white patches on his chest. It hasn't taken me long to decide that this cat is weird. Even my friend who has owned cats all her life says he's weird. I've named him Loopy because of his odd behaviour.

At night he runs around like a maniac, scrabbling at all the doors. He also likes to go outside at night and meow until someone lets him in, (we have a cat door but he won't use it at night). If you don't let him in, he climbs the door and hangs on the window at the top to peek inside.

Also, he only drinks water from running taps, and prefers that to his bowl. One of our bathrooms has a sink with a tap that it permanently dripping, (I know it will only take replacing the washer to fix it but I'm lazy like that). He spends much of the day sitting in this sink and catching the water in his mouth if he's thirsty.

Loopy also likes to sneak up on us when we are eating food. He'll hover by the table and wait until we are not watching and then he'll grab food off our plates and run away with it. He begs like a dog if we won't let him snatch our food and makes loud complaining noises if we ignore him.

Freddy's Lesson
Leslie, 36

I have a cat called Freddy who was always jumping onto the kitchen work tops and sniffing and licking any food that he found there.

One day I left some seriously hot chillies on the chopping board as I was cooking. I left the room to answer the door and Freddy jumped up to investigate my ingredients once again. I heard a yowl from the kitchen and ran back there; Freddy had apparently licked up a bit of chilli. He leapt off the work top, running over the chopping board and chillies as he went. He then did that classic 'embarrassed cat' thing, and began licking his paws. Of course there was chilli on them as well and he fled out the door into the garden. He never jumped onto the workplace again.

The only problem is that he now gets into a furious mood when I'm in the kitchen cooking. He literally races around the house. As he goes, things fall off shelves and cushions are scattered everywhere. Sometimes I have to shut all the doors and leave him in the hallway just to keep my rooms safe.

The Thief
Jan, 35

My grandmother likes to call my cat Lady, "the thief". Lady's fourteen years old, but she acts like she's a young thing. She's a huntress, though thankfully there haven't been too many mice left on our floors.

While my daughters were in primary school, she would sit at the breakfast table with me and my daughters as if it were her breakfast time, too. She was waiting to drink the milk my daughters would leave in their cereal bowls. Then, she seemed to grow out of the sitting at the table thing when we stopped having cereal every morning, so we figured our food was safe on the table.

It was for a while; we seemed to be able to leave anything out. However, one Sunday we left a chicken pie on the table overnight and discovered cat-sized bites had been taken out of it in the morning. We've now gone back to making sure that everything is put away out of reach of naughty paws.

Hungry the Cat
Caroline, 24

My Auntie Pat had a huge black cat called Hungry because from being a kitten he had always been obsessed about food. Hungry lived with Auntie Pat and my cousin Sara but the whole family loved him.

Hungry was the sweetest cat I've ever met. He would do all sorts of tricks to make us laugh and loved to be cuddled and be petted. Auntie Pat loved cats and started to feed a tortoiseshell cat that came to her back door. Eventually, this cat was named Sweetie and more or less moved in with Auntie Pat, Sara and Hungry. I don't know why they named her Sweetie because she clearly had an attitude problem. She was always hissing and clawing at everyone. Even Hungry was scared of her, despite being nearly twice her size.

Eventually the two got used to each other and a couple of times we'd catch them grooming each other. Sweetie had been pregnant when she turned up at the kitchen door and gave birth to her kittens behind the tumble drier one night. Hungry sat beside her watching over Sweetie and her kittens until Auntie Pat got up and moved Sweetie and her kittens to a basket in the downstairs bathroom. As the kittens got older, Hungry loved playing with them. He would chase them all over the house and they would clamber onto his back whenever he lay down.

Not long after this, Hungry began to lose weight and seemed unwell. The vet diagnosed a kidney stone and gave him some injections. Slowly he began to heal. He began to get his weight back and seemed much more like his usual self.

About a year later, Hungry began losing weight again and wouldn't eat much. He stopped playing and just lay on the floor all day, trying to stay somewhere where he wouldn't be disturbed. One day Auntie Pat found him under the bed, he wasn't breathing and we think he had died at some point during the night. The following Saturday I was with my cousin Sara in her room and we were reminiscing about Hungry and talking about how much we missed him.

Sara told me that during the night after Hungry died she was laying in bed not able to sleep, still sad over his death. She suddenly felt Hungry walking on her bed and on her legs, just like he used to do when he was alive and wanted to cuddle next to you to sleep.

Sara said she was a bit freaked out to see the blankets move and feel Hungry's paws but it was also comforting. I think Hungry loved being in that house so much that he couldn't bear to leave.

When Cats Choose Their Owners

Some cat lovers have the distinct impression that their cats think they own them, rather than the other way around. In this section we have included tales of the new cat in the house and how they got along with their new housemates.

Story of a Charmer
Petra, 51

I was never that keen on cats because I had never lived with one and thought that they were cold, unfriendly animals. That was until one decided to move into my house.

I had just got home from a friends' barbeque in late August and the sun was beginning to set behind my garden. As I took off my shoes a movement caught my eye in the kitchen. My heart began beating quickly and I feared that I had burglars. I picked up my long umbrella from the hall and cautiously made my way into the kitchen. It was then that I saw a large ginger cat sitting in the middle of the kitchen floor. I stared at it, ginger cat stared back. I realised that he must have got in through the open window by climbing up the fence then jumping through into the kitchen. I opened the door to get rid of him but he remained sitting in the middle of the kitchen. I made to push him out but he just yawned and settled down in a ball on the floor. Not knowing what to do I put down a saucer of milk for him and went off to watch TV.

By the time I wanted to go to bed, I tried again to get him out of the kitchen. I opened the door and made encouraging noises to get him to leave. He ignored me completely and eventually I went to bed.

The next morning he began rubbing around my legs and purring as I made some coffee. Then he became more brazen and began meowing loudly to indicate that I should give him some food. I didn't have any cat food so I gave him a tin of tuna fish and that seemed to satisfy him When I was ready to go to work I tried to get him out of the house again. This time he just walked past me into the sitting room. Worried about toilet troubles I put a few sheets of newspaper into an old washing up bowl and put it next to the kitchen door. There was nothing else for it, as I had to get to work.

When I got home, ginger cat was still there. He had used my improvised litter tray and was now clearly waiting for his supper. I gave him some milk and tried to find something that he could eat. The only thing I had to give him was a piece of frozen cod. I grilled it, left it to cool and then cut it up and put it on a plate for him. He ate it greedily and then followed me into the sitting room where he climbed onto my sofa and went to sleep. I watched him for a while and then made a decision. I would put up some "Cat Found" posters of him and in the meantime I would get some cat food and cat litter and look after him. I took my car keys and left him sleeping. Later that night, I tried to see once again if he wanted to leave but he wouldn't even come out into the hallway. I put out the cat litter and some food and went to bed.

After a few weeks of this I realised that no one was going to claim this cat and he had clearly decided to live with me. I called him Chancer because of the way he had come into my life and he lived with me for the next seven years. I had a cat door put into my back door so that he could come and go. He was happy to go outside if he knew that he could get back in. He eventually died in his sleep and I was so sad to lose him. I realised that I had become a cat lover and now I know that I will always have a cat in my life.

Adopted
Duncan, 44

Six years ago I was in a car accident which left me paralyzed from the waist down and severely depressed due to my resulting handicap. I had to move back home with my family, but they find me a burden and I don't really have friends in the area any more. It was a very lonely period as I endured a lot of pain during my long, slow recovery. One morning, the most lovable black and white stray cat appeared from nowhere and decided to adopt me by giving me a cheery meow and sauntering straight into our kitchen while the door was open. That was the start of a long relationship that enriched my life beyond words. Coco, as I called her, has given me unconditional love, and I think she has been a more beneficial therapy than any doctor or hospital could provide. Regardless of my traumas or depressed states I have always found true joy in caring for and providing for my beloved cat. In return, she has always been there to comfort me and be my companion. Loving and being with my cat has given me a quality of life that I thought would be impossible.

Stray Mum
Dave, 32

I used to feed the odd stray cat by our kitchen door. I would always save table scraps for them if there were any left over. One morning I opened the door and found a ginger and white cat sitting slightly further away from the two cats that I usually fed. She looked at me and I noticed that she was very pregnant.

As soon as I put the food into the tray outside the door she sprang forward and ate all the food almost without stopping for breath. I tried to take the tray away but she hissed at me and showed her teeth. The same thing happened when I put food out in the evening. I tried to stroke her but she would strike out with her claws to push my hand away. All she wanted was the food. Eventually, the other two strays moved on. The pregnant cat came for about two weeks and because of her predicament I took pity on her and tried to befriend her but she wouldn't let me touch her.

One night after I had been feeding her for a couple of weeks, there was a tremendous thunderstorm. There was really heavy rain with strong winds and fearsome lightning. I was in the kitchen looking out into the garden when I heard a meowing coming from outside the kitchen door. When I opened it there was the ginger and white cat walking around and shouting at me. She looked very scared and much thinner and as I watched she ran up the garden path, looking over her shoulder and meowing insistently to see if I was following. I grabbed my rain coat from the peg and ran after her.

She ran to a little bush by the garden fence and seemed to burrow into it. When I bent down to look I saw two tiny newborn kittens. I was quite frightened of her anger and her claws but I gently scooped up the kittens and headed back to my house. Ginger and white mum followed.

The cat stopped at the first door and refused to come all the way inside, preferring to stay sheltered in the porch. I didn't have time to argue with her, so I closed the outer door, leaving her in the porch. I went to the bathroom and towel dried the kittens but they were not moving. Then I picked up the hair dryer and put it on low, wafting it over them for a few minutes. Gradually, one of them started to wriggle. After another couple of minutes, the other kitten began to respond too and they both began squeaking.

I got out an old laundry basket and put a towel inside it for comfort and warmth and, after putting the two babies inside, carried it all downstairs. I put the basket down in the porch by mum and she immediately climbed into the bed with them and began to inspect them.

After she was convinced they were unharmed, she gave me a look of contentment and let me stroke her on the head, without hissing or lashing out. The kittens began to feed as she groomed them.

By morning the garden was so water-logged that I'm sure the kittens would have drowned if they had stayed where they were. I went out and bought some cat food for mum cat before work and put it on a saucer next to her. By evening she was happy to be moved into the kitchen where it was warmer. The kittens stayed with us until they were ten weeks old when they were adopted by some friends. Their mum lives with us still!

King Leo
Carol, 37

I live in a very rural area and people are always dropping off their unwanted pets in the woods behind my house. It makes me really angry because it seems such a cruel thing to do. I have had to take many dogs and cats to the local pet rescue centre because I worry about them starving to death in the winter.

One abandoned pet was a cat. One day I saw her carrying a little orange ball in her mouth. That same day a couple of hours later I couldn't help but notice an incessant high pitched mewing. After investigation I found that little orange ball beside my house. It was a tiny male kitten with scabs all over him. I took him to the vet and was told that he was only about two weeks old. I fed him (he was very violent at first. I had many scratches on my fingers from holding his baby bottle).

Now though, he is the king cat. I called him Leo and he is adorable. He likes to chase leaves, bask in the sun, and jump up on the kitchen work surfaces when I'm cooking; particularly if I'm preparing meat or fish. He's quite naughty but always entertaining.

I definitely didn't choose him, but I am glad that I have kept him.

Smokey's Hotel
Diane, 40

A few years ago, we went on holiday to a small Greek island. From the moment that the plane touched down we knew we were going to have a wonderful holiday. It was a lovely rural island with pine-covered mountains and lush olive groves. Lots of people had orange and peach trees in their gardens and you could see the delicious fruit hanging from them.

Our hotel was in a remote village between a donkey farm and an olive grove and we savoured the peace because back home we live in a large busy city. When we arrived we were shown to our room and were delighted to discover that it had two balconies, one overlooking the sea and the bay and the other looking out over an olive grove.

The balcony that looked over the olive grove had grape vines growing from the room below up a trellis, which ended at our balcony. We opened all the balcony doors to let the summer air in and settled down to have a cup of tea after our long journey. I opened a wardrobe door only to find out that we had another guest in our room. A grey and white tabby cat was asleep on the spare blankets inside. He didn't seem surprised to see me, he just yawned and came sauntering out into the room.

He went and sat by the fridge clearly indicating that he was hungry. Since we had only just arrived, we didn't have much to give him but we did have some milk to make tea with and so we gave him a saucer of that. He lapped it up and then went and lay down on one of the beds.

We called him Smokey and he spent the next two weeks living with us. We bought him tins of sardines and tuna and fed him everyday. Even if he'd gone out he always got back in by climbing up to the balcony along the grape vines. He was so calm and friendly it was hard to believe he was a stray cat, but he obviously was.

When we left to go home we had quite a sad goodbye but Smokey seemed to be fine with it. He was probably just going to go and wait in the wardrobe for the next guests!

Cat Nurse
Allie, 25

My grandma always had a cat. If she didn't have one, a cat soon found her. I remember her once coming home from the restaurant with a box of chicken. She put it down on the doorstep to open the door and saw something jump into the box. She picked it up (with whatever was inside still in it), and brought it into the kitchen. When she opened the box she found a very pregnant grey cat happily chewing on a chicken wing.

From then on, grandma would carry out a little food to her every day. To show her appreciation she patrolled around my buggy as if to prevent anything from hurting me. If someone came to visit, she stayed between me and the guest, they were not allowed near me! After her kitten was born, she brought her baby to see me and my grandma. Mummy cat let the kitten eat first and then she ate what was left. If a stray cat came, she made it clear to them. Kitten ate first. Then she and stray ate what was left. She always knew when I was tired or upset and would come to gently purr at me and rub her ears against me to make me feel better.

Both the grey mummy cat and the black kitten stayed with me and my grandma for the rest of their lives.

Betty the Stray
Ben, 34

I am now on my third cat. She is a female tabby, called Betty, and is now about seven years old. I found her near the industrial estate where I work. She had somehow set up home in an abandoned shop and I used to see her through the window wandering through the discarded shelving units and sometimes in the window. At first I gave her treats such as some milk or a bit of fish during my lunchtime walks, and she gradually began to trust me and would run into the empty shop window just in time to catch me as I walked past on my way to work.

Eventually, I took her home to my flat where she seemed content to settle, with a preference for pulling down towels from the heated towel rail in the bathroom, to use to make a sort of nest. I have to say that I was surprised when I came back from work about two weeks later to find that she had given birth to four kittens! From having no cats, I now had five.

I found good homes for all the kittens and, of course, took Betty to the vets to have her spayed. I didn't want any more surprises. Betty doesn't seem to mind. She's very content to be mostly an indoor cat. I think she might still remember what being out on the street without a home felt like. She still pulls down the warmed towels though. She's even worked out how to open the bathroom door when I try to keep it shut to stop her going in.

Abandoned Cats
Colin, 27

I have a cat that basically muscled her way into my life and then refused to leave. My next door neighbour moved out and left behind their cat and her two kittens.

I wasn't sorry to see them go, as they were neighbours from hell. They did some building work on their property that caused severe subsidence in our house. At one point I couldn't open my front door because the doorframe had shifted. But I still didn't think they would be so heartless as to abandon their pets. I couldn't believe it when I found out.

I didn't know what they'd done until about two days after they moved when I could hear cats meowing and saw one of them in the window. I knew that the house was empty as I had seen the moving vans. Not knowing what else to do, I went around to the back of their house and broke a pane of glass in the kitchen door so that I could get inside. I can't believe they just left these three cats locked in the house when they left – they would have starved if we hadn't let them out.

To start with they wouldn't come near me and I thought I would just have to let them make their own way. So I just put a bowl of food and a bowl of water down for them, and left them to it.

But pretty soon all three of them turned up on my doorstep and set up a cacophony of meowing. The mother cat banged at the door with her body and meowed incessantly for twenty-four hours demanding food while her kittens played with each other. She was a grey tabby cat and one of her kittens was black and white and the other was a stripy orange cat. None of them were looking in great shape. The mother was extremely thin and her kittens looked as if they had fleas. Still, I took to putting out food whilst I decided what to do about them.

I might not have paid much attention to the mother cat and should have taken her and her kittens to a rescue centre, but she had something different about her that drew me to her. When I put down food she nudged her kittens over to eat the food first. Then she would give me a meow and eat the remaining food. It was as if she was aware that I didn't have to feed them but had chosen to do so. I knew that if I took them to the animal rescue centre, the kittens might have a chance for adoption, but I was afraid that that the mother would probably end up being put down. I decided to adopt her, and to try to find homes for her kittens.

Finding homes for the two little kittens was relatively easy. I found a family just up the road who were so susceptible to cute, helpless little kittens that they took in both of them. I had decided to call the mother cat Jeanie and when the kittens had been taken by their new owners, I reassured her that they would be well looked after and gave her a tin of salmon as a treat.

At first Jeanie wasn't the sort of cat you could cuddle. She was happy to eat food that I put out but not so happy if I tried to stroke her. She often responded to strokes with a hiss and a lashing out of her claws. I also had to get her sorted out. She needed treatment for fleas and worms and I knew that I also needed to get her spayed.

Jeanie's first visit to the vet earned her the reputation of an aggressive little feline. She fought the vet and his assistant and I had to try to help to hold her down. By the time the appointment was over, the vet looked shell-shocked and his assistant had a large rip down the front of her apron. Jeanie had reacted badly to having her temperature taken and retched in fury when given a worm pill. I had to book an appointment to have her spayed and the vet told me I'd have to be there to hold her down when the anaesthetic was being administrated.

Still, once that whole ordeal was over she brightened up a bit. For the first couple of months she virtually ignored me except for ordering her meals and refused to behave like a pet cat. Then, one day, she rubbed around my legs one morning in the kitchen. When I bent down to give her a tentative stroke, she began to purr. It was a pivotal moment. I had been worried that Jeanie was going to be too much trouble to keep. Maybe she sensed it but, just when I was thinking about finding her a different home, her reaction to me changed.

Gradually it was as if I'd got a completely different cat. She became so affectionate, waiting behind the door to greet me, and curling up on the sofa with me. I am now allowed to stroke her as much as I want and she loves having her ears tickled. Jeanie spends her days purring, sleeping, and snuggling up to me and we couldn't be happier.

Pixie the Kitten
Dorothy, 43

We adopted a stray kitten. Well, if I'm honest, I think he adopted us. His mother was a stray cat who we saw taking her litter through our garden and Pixie was the tiny one who seemed to get left behind. He climbed up the apple tree by our back door. The next morning he was at the back door crying for food. We gave him some ham out of a can. He was an all black kitten with big yellow eyes. We all loved him from the start.

Pixie was very demanding straight away. He was always begging for food. If he'd eaten all the food in his bowl he would start panicking as if he thought that there would never be any more food available. We had to leave him food out all the time. As most cats do, he loved to rub against your shoes and legs when he wanted something. The rest of the time he liked to sleep in warm spots around the house.

Our next door neighbours had a dog that absolutely hated Pixie. He would sit on the fence calmly watching the dog try to jump up and get him. He never seemed scared of him though; I think that he would have liked to be friends with him.

Pixie's quite an old cat now and he doesn't seem as agile as he once did. The dog next door is long gone anyway. At fifteen, Pixie sleeps a lot more than he used to. I often find myself worrying about him because I can't imagine being without him.

Angry Cat
Ben, 27

I met a cat, one night recently whilst walking home from a party. He seemed to be very friendly, running right up to me and meowing, even rubbing against my leg. I talked to him and stroked him and I thought that we were getting along great.

As I set off to continue my journey home the cat began to follow me. I turned back to discourage him from following me and getting lost and without warning, he became very aggressive and attacked

77

me. He clawed at the backs of my legs and hissed at me furiously. Eventually I got away and looking back I could see the little thing sitting on the pavement watching me. I still have no idea what made him so angry. Perhaps he wanted to come home with me.

My Cat Cory
Colin, 72

Cory used to love lounging amongst the mint plants in my garden. When he went outside that is mostly what he did. He never went much further than our garden boundaries. He was happiest at the weekends or during the holidays when I could go outside and play with him. During warm summer evenings I would take my after-work beer out into the garden and sit feeding him salted popcorn, a snack that he absolutely loved.

He was especially fun when I had people round who didn't like cats. He was so persistent that he almost always won them over. He also couldn't stand other cats – ANY other cat. Hopeful visitors to our garden would be chased away with a stern warning wail.

I got him one day when I went to a barbecue at a friend's house further up the lane. Their neighbour's cat had had kittens and they had just started to venture away from their mother and explore the neighbourhood. As I was sitting in my chair sucking on a chicken leg a small kitten flung itself at my trouser leg and shimmied up as if it was a tree. It then proceeded to attach itself to my chest and wave a vaguely hopeful paw at the meat I was eating. I broke a bit off, gave it to him and our friendship was sealed.

The neighbours told us that the kittens were available for adoption if we wanted one and right there and then I agreed to take home a little animal that was to become my friend for the next sixteen years. He ran to the door every time the doorbell went to see who it was. Even if they had come to visit me he made sure to make it clear to them that to him, they had come to visit him and he would climb up their legs and sit on their chests until they acknowledged him and gave him a tickle behind the ears. He used to follow me to the pub in the evenings and wait outside until I had finished. If he thought it was getting too late he would run into the pub when the door opened and make a fuss in the bar until I drank up and went home. All the neighbours knew him and he was known as such a character in our village.

Around sixteen years after I first brought him home I woke up one morning and Cory was lying still on the kitchen floor. He was still breathing but he seemed so weak and made no attempt to run up to me and start to order breakfast. I took him to the vet who examined him and told me that it was just old age and the best I could do was take Cory home and keep him warm and comfortable. He had become much thinner and was relatively light for me to carry by then. He died about four days later.

I missed him so much but my friends in the village were very kind to me and helped to get me through it. A little wreath was left by some of the villagers on our green with a remembrance card, it was very touching.

Our vicar allowed him to be buried by my family's grave at the end of a row in the churchyard and one day I know I'll be there with him again.

Cats with Attitude

Cats are well known for being aloof and for having a bit of an attitude – for those who don't like them this is a disadvantage, but for many cat lovers it is part of the appeal. Here we find stories of feline bad behaviour, including cats that climb curtains, hide in cupboards, cats that like to walk alone, steal biscuits, or that simply won't be told.

Under the Covers
Kelvin, 31

I used to have a Siamese cat who insisted on getting into bed with me every night. Most cats I know sleep on top of the bed but this one snuggled down under the duvet with his head on my pillow. I had to hug him close like he was a teddy bear or he wriggled until he was pressed up against you. It was a nightmare on rainy days because wet or dry it was the same routine; pushing his way under the covers all spiky wet hair and muddy paws.

He would get into any bed in the house so long as it was occupied so I used to warn house guests about him and told them to shut their doors of they didn't want a furry friend visiting in the middle of the night.

I've still never met another cat who thought that it was normal to sleep under the covers like humans do.

The Cat Burglar
Joanna, 42

I had wanted a pet cat since I was a young child but my mother wouldn't allow it. Instead I had a part-time cat called Henry who lived next door and would come to visit me in our yard where I'd try to keep him as long as possible by bribing him with milk and tasty snacks.

When I was in my twenties, I moved into a flat with a boyfriend who would eventually become my husband. One night in a local bar I was talking to a friend of a friend who said that he was looking for a home for two kittens who had been living in his basement. I was in a cheerful mood so I readily agreed to take on the homeless kittens. The next day he brought them round and my life of looking after cats began.

From the outset both kittens were lively and friendly, but it was the male kitten, who I called Barney, that entertained me the most during the first weeks of us being housemates. He was a very sturdy kitten, almost like a tiny bear. His fur was white with two distinct black shapes on his back, a large "U" shape and above that a triangle. He also had a little cap of black fur above his white face.

We had a drawstring bag hanging on the back of the kitchen door where we kept plastic carrier bags for re-cycling. Barney loved to get into the bag and swing in it as though it were a huge hammock. He also spent a lot of time charging into cupboards. To tease him, I would shut the door as if I hadn't seen him go in there and then make noises as if I were dishing out his supper.

He'd squeak loudly until I opened the door to let him out.

At that time I wore a lot of silver jewellery, many earrings, bracelets and rings. I always took them off before going to bed and often left them in the sitting room by the fireplace. After a couple of weeks I realised that my silver jewellery was going missing. If I put a pair of silver earrings by the fireplace they would have gone in the morning. I was beginning to feel puzzled as to what was happening. Was I losing my memory? Had I lost them outside somehow? Eventually, it became clear that my jewellery really was vanishing.

I was home one afternoon when I heard a sort of jingle and rattling sound coming from the hall. Barney had his paw inside one of my boots that I had left by the door. He seemed to be trying to get something out of it. When I picked it up and shook out the contents several items of my silver jewellery fell out. Immediately he picked an earring up in his mouth and ran into the kitchen where he attempted to put it behind a cupboard. I found more jewellery behind cupboards and more still in other shoes. Little Barney was like a magpie. Every time I took off a piece of jewellery, he would pick it up and carry it somewhere else. It seemed that his favourite thing was to drop it into a pair of my boots and then scrabble around inside with his paws to try to get it out again. Whenever I lost an item of jewellery I would have to look inside all boots and shoes and behind cupboards; my little cat was a thief.

I shared my home with Barney for the next thirteen years. He continued to steal things occasionally, hair bands, small scarves and gloves. One time he came home with a still warm fish finger in his mouth. Both our neighbours had small children, but I'm still not sure how Barney got it and why he brought it home instead of eating it where he found it. It was as if he wanted to bring it home to show me what a good thief he was. I already knew that!

Little Star
Jane, 38

I have a lot of cats but little Star is my favourite. She is a tortoiseshell with an attitude like a fire cracker. She is the sort of cat that follows you around everywhere and she knows when I am feeling sad or worried. She watches me when I have a shower and meows as if she is very concerned about it, given that she can't stand getting wet. If she brings me a 'present' like a dead bird or mouse she is furious if I don't look pleased with it.

Sometimes she falls asleep on top of the dresser but then always stretches in her sleep, so she often falls off it. Every time that happens, if I am in the room she will glare at me like it's my fault and then avoid me all day by running away every time she sees me.

Star likes to stick her face into every bag in the house including those belonging to guests or workmen. If I move furniture she quickly lets me know that she is not happy about it. She is the most amazing cat because you always know exactly what she's thinking and there's never a dull moment with her.

Who Owns This House, Anyway?
James, 42

My cat Jimmy always lets us know when he is annoyed. He has a special "I'm annoyed", meow. The computer chair belongs to him and him alone, if you try to push him off it he refuses to move and sometimes even growls at you. I often end up just rolling it aside and using a kitchen chair instead, so I can get some work done.

He also owns the rug in the bedroom, our daughter's bed and the space under the lavender bush in the garden. If someone rings the doorbell, he will always be the first to the door as if it's his house.

I sometimes wonder if he thinks he pays the mortgage.

Rory and Rusty
Pat, 63

I have two male cats called Rory and Rusty. They're brothers and are both ginger stripy cats. They are forever getting into trouble. If there is anything on any surface in the house they will knock it off by pushing at it. I've had to give up having any breakable ornaments because they will inevitably get broken by one of my cats. Rusty likes to lie flat on his stomach like a slug. He will also pick something up with his mouth and then climb up onto any table or work surface and then immediately push it off onto the floor with his paws. Rory has a piece of string that is his favourite toy; he drags it behind him and then stops and chases it. If Rusty tries to chase it, Rory will drop the string and glare at him to let him know whose string it is. Rory waits in the bathroom for me to get out of the shower. Then he starts to lick my feet and rub his face and head all over them. He also likes to wake me up in the middle of the night by purring and rubbing against my face. They are both very lovable cats even when they're being a nuisance.

Feisty
Dan, 31

I once had a Siamese cat called Feisty who would only eat a certain brand of cat food. If I tried to give him something else he would either sniff it and walk away, or just remain sitting on the kitchen floor without even looking at it. Maybe he could smell that it wasn't the right brand. He would often get into tantrums, running round the kitchen work surfaces and pushing things off shelves with his paws just to show me how angry he was. Sometimes, he would go outside and return with an old chicken bone from somewhere which he would put down in front of me as if to say, "You eat that then"!

He was very fond of bringing disgusting bits of food from other people's rubbish into the house if he didn't like his food. It was as if he was trying to tell me how disgusting the food I'd tried to give him was. He was always very interactive and picky, which is why he was called Feisty, but it was the food or rather the quality of it that he was the most obsessed with.

Mercer and Slinky
Sally, 27

We have a cat called Mercer who used to be really aggressive. Even when you played with him you would end up with so many bite marks and scratches on you that you looked like you'd fallen into a bramble bush.

When he was about three we got a little grey female kitten who he really took to. We called her Slinky because she was such a beautiful colour and so elegant. Mercer began to keep an eye on her when they were in the garden. If she climbed too high up a tree he would start meowing as though he was worried that she might get into difficulties.

Slinky has completely changed Mercer's personality. He's a much gentler cat now than he's ever been.

Bee Trouble
Bethany, 25

My cat is called Bee because she has such beautiful stripy markings that make her look a little bit like a bumblebee. When she was a kitten she was tiny and the stripes were so bold that they looked as if they were painted on. She's quite small, short-haired and, in my opinion, the best cat in the world.

She sleeps with me every night, and follows me around the house when I'm home. She can be quite a problem in the night though as she likes to sleep on top of me and if I change position in my sleep she will jump off me with a kick that wakes me up. Then she climbs back on me again and it's hard to get back to sleep. She doesn't really like cuddling, but can sometimes get suddenly affectionate, and then forces me to give her all of my attention whatever I'm doing at the time. She is a nuisance, but I love her so much. Cats are wonderful animals.

The Electric Blanket
Lily, 25

My cat Carly doesn't like to sleep on the bed. Not unless it's particularly cold. This year however, things have changed a bit because I've bought an electric under blanket to keep me warm. Suddenly she absolutely loves getting on the bed as I read before going to sleep. It's almost impossible to get her off.

Her discovery of the electric blanket has meant that Carly has also learnt the fine art of subtly pushing me over so that she gets more heat to herself. I often wake up and find myself in the cold part of the bed at night.

She's a very sneaky cat.

Crazy Sushi
Helen, 29

Before I got my current Siamese cat Sushi, I used to have a much more laidback cat so I really notice how crazy Sushi's behaviour is.

Sushi tries to wake me up in the night or early morning by standing on my face, using all four paws! That's his peak time for wanting attention, food, and entertainment. It's as if he is training me to give him what he wants when he wants it. I have to ignore him or I'll be woken up every night forever. I know it will take time but hopefully he will learn he has nothing to gain by waking me up and will eventually stop.

Sushi also likes to sleep in the bath. I would have though that it would be too cold and uncomfortable but he seems happy there. If I use the bathroom in the night he is all stretched out looking pleased with himself.

During the day he gets into my desk drawer when I'm working from home and pulls at the lead on the back of the mouse so I can't move it. No attempts at persuading him to get out of the drawer have ever worked and it's too small a gap for me to get him out of it. He only comes out if I make a sandwich, especially a tuna one, and offer him a bit.

He hides shoes and steals socks; he even growls when the doorbell rings. Plastic bags infuriate him and he's always attacking them, biting and dragging them round the kitchen. He likes cucumber and always jumps up onto the kitchen counter top if I'm cutting one. I've found him hiding in the airing cupboard, under the cooker and once inside the lining of a coat; he had ripped the lining with his paws and slipped inside. Sushi really is completely nuts.

Evil Genius
Wendy, 40

My cat Charcoal is an evil genius. When we got him as a greyish black ten-week-old kitten he decided that he ruled the house straight away. He climbed into the dresser drawers from the back of it and explored everything he could. He attacked shoes and anything that moved. The, one day we realised that he had one funny little habit that we hadn't noticed.

My son collects bottle tops from a particular brand of beer. He puts them in a dish on a shelf in his room and he started to notice that his collection was diminishing. He was in his room reading one day when Charcoal sneaked in. Not thinking he was being watched, he jumped up onto the shelf and hooked a bottle top with his paw, pulling it out of the bowl. He then picked it up in his mouth and ran off with it.

My son followed and watched as Charcoal ran into the back garden and disappeared under the garage. When my son investigated he found a little heap of his bottle tops under the garage with a smug looking Charcoal sitting on top of them.

Poppy and Tinker
Sam, 34

I have had cats since I was small. When I was about seven, one of my cats had a litter of kittens. I remember how small and cute they were and how I cried when each of them went to their different homes.

I have two cats now, Tinker and Poppy. We got Tinker when one of my daughter's friends was moving house and they couldn't keep the cat. I am not sure of his age but I think he's between five and seven years old. Tinker immediately became part of our family. He has a voracious appetite and has always been a big solid cat.

Poppy has been with us since she was about twelve weeks old. One day, about two years ago, one of our neighbours' sons was coming door to door offering free kittens because his cat had just had a litter. My daughter, who was five years old at the time, begged and begged us to get her one and so we agreed that she could choose one.

She chose a tiny black and white female and called her Poppy because there is a flower-shaped patch on her back. Cats have their own unique personalities and are often quite funny. Poppy is very timid and runs and hides when anyone visits our house. It's as if she thinks that she is going to be snatched away. She is tiny and loves to purr. Her meow is very squeaky and it makes you laugh just to hear it. She loves our daughter very much and spends much of her time in her bedroom.

Tinker will come to you to be stroked, but always on his terms. Every time I try to tie my shoe laces, he attacks them. This can be annoying when I am in a hurry. If you try to pick him up he wriggles out of your arms like he's fighting to stay alive. He is not what you would call a "lap cat" but will sit by the side of you or above your head on the chair or the sofa.

Tinker is a bit of a drama queen and loves attention. He likes chewing blankets and shoes; a lot of our shoes have teeth marks on them. Sometimes he trots up to you and meows. He is very vocal and always has something to say. Poppy and Tinker get on well with each other and don't fight over places to sleep as I've seen some cats do. I think it's because they are such different characters they don't clash that often.

Master Freddie
Sara, 28

We have a young cat called Freddie. When he was a kitten he was absolutely crazy but as he's got a bit older he's become much quieter. Now he's so serious it's comical. I have taken to calling him Master Freddie.

When he was a kitten he would charge around the house tearing up the toilet paper, climbing up the plastic blinds on the windows, and sticking his little face into jars of pens and cups of coffee. He was a real little prankster.

Now he is terribly dignified. He likes to sit up like an Egyptian statue, or lie against my leg when I'm writing at my desk. Nevertheless, I still love him in all his moods. He is a black and white cat, more white than black. We are putting off neutering him in the hope that he'll turn into one of those big, fierce tomcats that I love so much.

He is very good at standing up to the other cats that come into our garden. One of them attacked him and he just growled at him and made a loud hissing, wailing noise. He's not scared of anything. Freddie is mostly an indoor cat, so I'm not worried about him wandering off. I worry about all the strays and if he was the sort of cat who likes to be outdoors most of the time I would have had him neutered.

Doglike
Katherine, 28

I have a cat called Bobbin who actually thinks he's a guard dog.

If he's in the garden and sees a cat or dog go past, he starts to growl and then chases them. I've also seen him chase a fox. He just goes mad and goes for them, and they look a bit surprised but trot away rather than confront him, luckily.

If the doorbell rings he growls and runs out into the hall. Visitors get him walking round and round their legs making a warning, growly, wailing noise.

I think he's threatening them to make sure they stay away from his food. He even trots like a dog.

Feuding Cats
Karl, 30

My cats Noah and Catkins have some sort of blood feud going on between them. They don't just stalk and fight each other like normal cats do. Instead they're like two small children; Noah will swipe at Catkins when he walks past. Catkins will wait an hour or two, and then slap Noah as he sleeps. Noah then waits a while, and jumps on Catkin while he's eating or drinking. And so it goes. Until they end up just slapping at each other like teenage girls.

After the slapping, things usually quieten down for a few hours, and Noah and Catkins lay off each other, although the loser of the slap fight usually takes it out on our pile of old newspapers in the kitchen. You can hear the frantic ripping sound from the sitting room.

Bouncing Beans
Neil, 27

I have a cat called Beans who is very bouncy. From the moment I took him home he has jumped on every surface in the house he can reach and you can see him standing on his little hind legs testing out how high the top of the wardrobe is to jump onto. (Too high!)

He is very adaptable and shows enthusiasm for every new situation. When I got a new rug, he jumped all over it and then lay on his side and pulled up the corners dragging himself round it with his claws. He also likes to jump up onto your shoulders from the ground, which is OK as long as you know what his intentions are. He loves to jump into boxes and in and out of bushes in the garden; something which could be startling if you didn't know he was out there.

He's quite good at catching things, probably because of his agility and he loves games where he can pounce on things dragged around the room. The only downside is that in the night he's worked out how to make a giant leap from the top of the dresser in the bedroom, right onto the bed. It's like someone throwing a heavy weight at you when you're asleep. It's no good trying to ban him from the bedroom either. He just throws himself at the door until you give in and open it.

Night Nuisance
Jeanette, 27

My cat Pollyanna is a small black cat with a white bib and she is truly bonkers. In the evening she tends to get very overexcited and starts to chase imaginary things around the house. Sometimes she goes in completely the other direction and imagines that someone or something is chasing her instead. She hides behind doors before peeping round them and then running away from whatever it is she's imagining lurking behind them.

During the night, she walks around my bed purring until I reach down, pick her up and put her onto the bed. She's a nuisance though, because she doesn't go to sleep like normal cats; she bounces around hiding under the covers, then scrabbling out of them and chasing round and round. Sometimes she gets into the wardrobe and you can hear her shuffling around amongst the shoes.

If you shut her out of the bedroom she makes such a racket outside the bedroom door that you have to get up and open it again.

Still, she is such a loving little cat that I'm prepared to tolerate a few sleepless nights. She's a little nuisance but a very lovable nuisance.

Shouty Cat and Shy Cat
Connie, 52

We have a holiday home in Spain, near to the southern end of the border with Portugal. It is a lovely place on the edge of a village on the mountainside, and I'm lucky to be able to go there from time to time.

Whenever I am there, there are two grey cats who turn up. I call them Shouty Cat and Shy Cat, for fairly obvious reasons. Usually Shouty Cat comes and weaves around my legs wheedling for food, while Shy Cat skulks a bit further away looking nervous, until I put some food down, at which point she overcomes her shyness and dashes in to grab a few mouthfuls.

I don't let them in the house, they usually show up on the veranda and as long as I am in the house they turn up every day at least once or twice. I'm not sure if they are strays or if they live with a family in the village. Quite often in Spain cats are neither totally stray or domesticated – they may be looked after and fed by one particular family, but stay outside the home and sleep in out-buildings or wherever they can find some shade.

A couple of months ago I went to the house and was quite worried about Shy Cat. Shouty Cat still turned up every day demanding food but there was no sign of Shy Cat. Finally on the Saturday, Shy Cat turned up at the usual time, but she wasn't alone. She had a tiny black kitten in her mouth. She put him down in the flowerbed, then disappeared into the field and came back three more times with kittens, until she had a whole litter, all different colours. Obviously she had decided that my veranda was a good place for them

They were beautiful little things; I think their eyes must only just have opened. She seemed positively proud of them and I spent a lot of time that week watching them play and learn to fight and walk.

I'm going back next week, so I will look forward to seeing how the kittens are getting on and if they are still living with their mother.

Sadie
Joanna, 26

I had always grown up with large dogs but when I left home I needed to get something smaller and so decided to get a kitten. There was a note in the local newsagent's window advertising kittens wanting good homes, so I called the number. The lady that answered was very nice but told me that most of the litter had already been placed with homes and the one remaining kitten, a little tabby and white female, was supposed to be given to a man who had been round the night before. She said that if he hadn't contacted her within 24 hours, I could have that kitten if I wanted.

When the phone rang at the following evening, I rushed to answer, keeping my fingers crossed as I did so. It was good news. I could have the female kitten. I drove round to their house, stopping for some cat litter, a litter tray and some kitten food, and prepared to meet my new housemate.

I spotted the kitten as soon as the door opened. She had the sweetest little face and an endearing habit of putting her head on one side when she looked at you. She had a very high pitched meow that seemed to make her even smaller and I was so happy that she was to be mine. There was a brief good-bye to the lady of the house where she had been born and then we were off.

I've had Sadie for five months now and she's been so much fun. I've noticed that she steals things, or more correctly she carries things from room to room so that I can't find them. Last night I was getting ready to go out to dinner and I put in one hoop earring but when I reached for the other it had disappeared! I had to chase Sadie round the house to get her to give it back.

She is constantly playing, chasing things, or jumping in and out of cardboard boxes. The only times she seems to be remotely willing to chill out a bit is at night when she settles down on my bed. In theory I still live alone but it never feels like that anymore. I feel more as if I live with a colony of imps or a houseful of gremlins.

Cool Cat
Mark, 30

I have the coolest cat in the world. His name is Jimbo and he's a black cat with a little patch on his chest. He always comes when I call him, and he comforts me when I'm a bit down. He's straight onto my lap whenever it's available and when it's not he spends a long time trying to push his way onto it. He's brilliant at playing with the children even though my two-year-old is still learning to be gentle with him. He sits and lets her try to stroke him even when she's really tugging on his tail and quite often chases him. He's also got a little cat friend who comes to the kitchen door and meows for him. When I call for Jimbo to let him know his friend is here, he comes to the door and goes outside to play like a child. I think he thinks that he is as human as the rest of us.

Toby the Outdoors Cat
Ed, 27

I have a black cat called Toby, I think he was abused by someone before we got him. Their neighbours gave him to us, wanting to find him a good home after the original owners abandoned him, and he has become a part of our family. He's used to being a outdoors cat and hunting for his own food but I don't like him going outside as much in the winter as I do in the warm months and even then I don't want him out every day because I want to know he's OK. About two years ago he went missing for a couple of days and when he did come home he had a big wound (about an inch in diameter), in the upper muscle of his left leg. Fortunately for us, it healed up after about four weeks or so.

We live near a busy road junction, and for over two years he's avoided being hit by a car but sometimes he acts like he's invulnerable and can't be hurt. He seems to think that our street is his street and he crosses the road as slowly as he wants to, it really frightens me sometimes. Also, he will not allow another cat in his territory, if he finds one there, he'll go after it relentlessly until it leaves. We have a couple of regular cats that wander around our neighbourhood anyway, there's a ginger one that my cat absolutely hates but I've never seen them fight, I think the ginger cat just runs off at the sight of Toby, He does have fights with a black and white cat that is constantly trying to get into his territory. I was worried for a while that Toby was going to really hurt him but I think really he's just protecting his 'turf'.

Shadow
Flick, 21

My Siamese cat is called Shadow because she follows me everywhere. She makes me laugh all the time with her antics, for instance the way she stretches and rolls on the floor or bed or couch or chair. She also loves to chase us around the house.

One of her favourite things is to race up and down the stairs and then check to see if we're following. She puts her little face around the banister at the top of the stairs and meows if we're not chasing her. She's very vocal and talks all the time with meows of different length and tone. If she's in a different part of the house to us, she'll start meowing really loudly until someone comes to find her.

She's also an excellent mouser, though it's horrible disposing of her victims. She always lets us know when she's ready for her dinner, with a loud meow. She watches TV and gets up on the TV cabinet to examine things that interest her. I find myself talking to her a lot and I know she's listening because she usually answers me with some sort of meow noise.

I probably sound completely mad but I just really like my cat.

The Travelling Cat
Colleen, 71

When I was a little girl I used to get the bus to school. It was only a few stops, but the strangest thing was that a little tabby cat began to get on the bus at the stop where I got on and sit on the bus for precisely two stops before getting out again at the shops. For several months when I was ten years old this cat did this every day, always the same stop to get on and off the bus. In fact, it began to cause quite a stir in neighbourhood.

Eventually my next door neighbour, Mrs Burton, followed the cat off the bus to see where it went next and try to find out what it was doing. Along the small row of shops where the cat got off the bus, there was a fishmonger and Mrs Burton said that the cat went straight in there. A few minutes later the cat came out carrying a small white plastic bag in its mouth. It then moved fast, running back towards the place where it had got on the bus earlier.

Mrs Burton followed the cat to a garage behind an empty house that was for sale. Once there it tore the wrapping off the fish with its teeth and ate it. Our next-door neighbour investigated and found out that the cat had lived with an elderly lady until she died about eight months previously. Her children weren't interested in keeping the cat and had simply left him behind when they cleared out the house.

The fishmonger said that the cat used to travel with the old lady to his shop every day or so for some fish for herself and a bag of scraps for the cat. The cat, which was called Tiddly-Wink, used to sit in her basket. After she died, when Tiddly-Wink felt hungry he simply went to get food the only way he knew how; from the fishmongers.

The owner of the fish shop said that he had taken to keeping some scraps for the cat as he had always done. He had heard that the old lady had died but since the cat kept turning up in the mornings for something to eat he had kept handing over his scraps.

He hadn't realised that the cat had become a stray and when he found out, decided to adopt it. Tiddly-Wink became quite famous in our small town after that. If you went into the fishmongers he would often be sitting proudly on the front step, usually vigorously washing his whiskers.

Baby Love
Julie, 43

I once had a tortoiseshell cat called Stella who was very vocal and had no problem showing her emotions whether she was happy and purring or furious and in a bad mood. I had got her as a kitten when a friend of a friend moved into a house and found a cat with two kittens living in the garden. I agreed to take the kittens: Stella was the tortoiseshell female and the other kitten was her white and ginger brother. Stella was the sort of cat who would follow you from room to room; she loved to interact with you and would always respond if you spoke to her.

The cats had lived with us for about six years when I discovered that I was pregnant. My husband and I had been together for ten years and were both delighted at this new development and nine months later we arrived home from the hospital with our little baby daughter.

From the outset Stella was not very happy about our new "pet". It got more attention that she did and this was always going to be an issue. During the day our daughter slept in a Moses basket where I could keep an eye on her and Stella would walk round and round the basket staring into it with hugely dilated pupils. She would often give me a baleful look. I would feel guilty and play with her in the kitchen when my daughter was asleep to try and cheer her up. Although Stella was clearly happy to be played with you could tell that she was really jealous of the baby.

Whilst our daughter was a baby I used to work from home and my desk was near to the door that led into the hall. I kept a ready-packed baby bag out there that was always ready to go with nappies, creams and toys so that I could leave the house without too much fuss. One day, I was working at my desk when a movement from the hallway caught my eye. As I watched, Stella got on top of the baby bag and very deliberately, whilst looking me straight in the eye, she peed on the bag. It was such a clear message of "what I think about the arrival of our new creature". Because it was so clear that she was communicating with me I just watched incredulously at first then finally chased her off, emptied the bag and threw it into the washing machine.

Things calmed down a little after that. It was as if once Stella knew that she'd made her point she calmed down a bit. She never really got used to the baby, but she ended up tolerating her and would even let her pat her on the head occasionally, though mostly she would find the highest spot in the room to sleep in so she could feel safe from being chased by the little one.

Keyboard Trouble
Jon, 20

Bwqlf/;VNJ B.CLN 'ASM 'M' l'C;OHCOHE;xxx888888888PB 8qxjbnNNI;K9ejjsjcpwu09uujju90uf[0ufjcpkKCU9...

I did have a story but my cat won't get off the keyboard!

Cats and Other Animals

It's always interesting to see how different species of animals get along. In this section we include stories of cats and their relationships with dogs, birds and other animals in and around the house, some of which are friendly, some less so.

Sula the Sparrow Catcher
Cleo, 47

My cat Sula hated birds, or to put it another way she hated birds but took great pleasure in trying to rid the world of those nasty little flying creatures. I often had to get rid of dead birds or try to help the uninjured ones get away.

One night Sula came home with a sparrow. She let go of the bird to play with it and I could see that it was uninjured so I tried to catch it myself. The bird was flying around the kitchen, closely followed by me and my cat. I hoped I could get the bird out without the kitchen being destroyed.

Eventually the sparrow flew out from behind the washing machine and clung for dear life to a light fitting. I managed to grasp the bird from the floor in the corner before Sula could get to it. As

I lifted it, the little thing clung on to my finger and remained very still. I went through the flat to my front door and stood holding my finger (and the sparrow) away from me thinking that the bird would fly away.

However, it had gone catatonic and wouldn't move. It didn't even blink. It was a rainy evening and I was in my pyjamas standing at the top of my steps in the doorway with a sparrow on my finger. Passers by gave me curious glances but probably thought I had lost my mind and quickly walked by. I didn't know what to do to make the sparrow know it could fly away. It was getting later and wetter and so I gently lifted the tiny bird from my finger and put him onto the outside windowsill. As I was returning inside the house I saw it fly away. It had taken a long time but at least the bird was safe and free.

Cat s and Dogs...
Gillian, 21

When I was 14 years old I rescued a little ginger kitten from drowning. My best friend's cat, a spoilt Siamese called Chloe, had kittens but instead of them being all Siamese (and therefore worth some money), one came out with ginger stripes. Her dad was going to get rid of it by drowning it. I told him I wanted it and he told me I could have it.

I walked home with the kitten tucked into the front of my jacket, his little head poking out under my chin. It began to rain before I got home. My Mum had gone out so I waited in the garage until she got back. When my mum came home I walked out of the garage yard and showed her the tiny ginger kitten with the huge ears. Mum sighed and pointed out that our dog Hamish would probably try to kill it.

Hamish looked affronted when I set Ginger on the kitchen floor. He first of all gave a grunt and then went and stood protectively by his food bowl. Ginger wasn't perturbed and immediately walked up to Hamish to give him a sniff. Hamish sniffed the cat back and then they just stood staring at each other for a couple of minutes. Then Ginger shinned up Hamish's leg and clambered onto his back. Hamish first looked startled but then began to wag his tail and trot around the kitchen. Ginger sat on his back and held on.

From that day on, Hamish and Ginger became firm friends. All our neighbours would comment on the sight of a dog in our garden with a cat on its back. They even sleep together in Hamish's dog basket, because Ginger looked on the smaller basket that I got for him with utmost disdain. I've put soil and flowers in it now and put it in the garden.

It's very strange. I've never seen a dog and cat become so close.

Rabbit Watch
Kate, 34

I have a small home gym where I like to exercise on a rowing machine in the mornings. I came home from running some errands one day, and instead of running over to greet me like he usually does, my cat Toby was staring at my rowing machine. Intrigued, I went over to see what it was that had got him so interested. I caught a glimpse of a little bit of fur between the machine's base and the wall. At first, I thought that it was one of his toys…until it moved.

I was terrified that it was a rat and I'd have to catch it and set it free. I peered down the back of the rowing machine but couldn't see anything so I went about my day.

However, some time later I saw Toby staring at the rowing machine again and went over to see what he was looking at. This time I heard a weird crunchy noise and a little squeak. Going closer I looked underneath the machine. It was definitely something furry and alive. Not wanting to startle whatever it was in there I gently lifted up the rowing machine and saw a baby rabbit! I wasn't quite sure what to do with it but I managed to get it into a shoe box and take it into the garden where I set it free. I think it may have come in through the cat flap.

Later that evening my next door neighbour came around asking anyone if they had seen a baby rabbit because she had got one for her little boy. Thankfully, it was still wandering around nibbling the grass, so I was able to re-unite her with her tiny new pet. She thanked me and I told her how I had found it. Apparently she had opened the rabbit hutch to get it out and it had run off. At least now I know where to take it if it escapes again.

Angry Birds
Ruth, 32

I have a six-year-old tomcat called Rusty. We gave him that name because, although he's a black cat, in certain lights he looks sort of rusty brown. A couple of years ago he caught a starling in the garden. The bird immediately began to make the loudest squawking noise I've ever heard, and what happened next was very strange. Seemingly out of nowhere loads of starlings arrived and all made the same noise.

The roof of the house was covered in shouting starlings, so were our garden fences and then even more arrived and perched along the washing line. I was frightened that they all might attack him en masse so I went outside with a broom and poked Rusty with it until he let the starling go. Thankfully it was unharmed and it flew away. Once it had gone all the other starlings began to fly away too. It must have made some impression on Rusty because he's never gone after a starling since.

Found by a Dog
Bella, 23

One morning in the summer I was having breakfast outside on the patio when my dog Scotty walked over to a bush and began to paw at the ground whilst making an odd whining noise. I called him back but he ignored me and simply lay down on the lawn continuing to whimper. I decided to go and see what it was that had caught Scotty's attention. I bent down and looked under the bush, and saw a tiny kitten staring back at me with bright yellow eyes. I was surprised she hadn't run off at the sight of Scotty but perhaps she was scared to move in case he went for her. I sent Scotty back into the kitchen so he wouldn't frighten the kitten

She meowed at me as I lay down to get a closer look at her. I was worried that she might be stuck or injured but when I said hello she meowed back at me. I looked around to see if there was a mother cat anywhere nearby but I couldn't see another cat and I knew that none of my neighbours has a cat. I reached for her and although she tried to wriggle away, I got my hand around her and gently held onto her as I backed out from under the bush. I decided that I would feed her and also put some food outside to try to encourage her mum to show up.

I stood up and held her up to get a good look at her, and my first thought was "what a pretty little face"! Then I noticed that one of her back legs hung limp. Hoping I was wrong I set her down to see if she could stand. And she immediately listed sideways. There was no time to waste; I had to get this kitten to the vet as soon as possible.

I wrapped her in a soft cardigan and got into the car to take her to my local vets. She didn't make a fuss; she just sat there staring at me with her yellow eyes. The vet decided to keep her in to set her leg and said that he would sedate her to stop her trying to move so much. She gave me another little meow as I left.

Three days later I collected her from the vet and she looked much perkier. Her leg was still bandaged but she could manage to walk a little. I put a litter tray in the kitchen so that she didn't have to go outside and I gave her a saucer of warm milk which she lapped up greedily. After that she came to me and purred and I knew that we were going to be great friends.

I called her Blossom because I found her under a rhododendron bush and it had large crimson flowers all over it. Blossom has been with me for three years now. Her leg mended and she became a little scamp of a cat. Always chasing Scotty or jumping into mischief. I'm so glad she came into my garden that day.

Monkey Cat
Paula, 34

When my cat Eddie was a kitten he had a little monkey toy that made a sound like a monkey chattering. Whenever the monkey talked, Eddie would talk back to it in a funny voice. The monkey toy was chewed to bits years ago but Eddie still makes the funny chattering sound to me. The other thing he does is, when I'm giving him his food in the morning, he gets so excited that he starts eating anything around him; carpet, dust, the rug, our old newspapers.

It's as if he's chewing in anticipation of getting his meal. He also likes to drink from the bathroom sink instead of his water bowl. He meows and I have to go into the bathroom and turn the tap on. If I don't, he goes on the rampage around my bathroom, knocking things like soap, hairspray, toothpaste and toothbrushes, onto the floor.

Skittle the Bird Hater
Rose, 32

I used to have three cats but my youngest one, Zara, got lost so now I just have the two. The oldest is a black male called Charlie, and he's very shy and only goes as far the garden fence. He prefers to sleep on the lawn rather than roam the wilderness. My other cat is a tortoiseshell female called Skittle. She's very confident and bold. She loves to sleep and eat, but spends most of her time outside hunting for small birds and animals.

Because Skittle likes to go outside, she gets into the most adventures. She absolutely hates birds and if she sees one, she makes a "Kak, kak, kak" noise and flings her tail about.

If cats really do have nine lives, you can be sure she must have used them all up by now, yet she's only six years old. She once spent the night outside during a very bad storm. By midnight, she still had not come home so I took a flashlight and went out to look for her. I found her under a tree hiding because she hates getting wet. I picked her up and put her inside my raincoat to take her safely home. When we got home Charlie went to have a sniff at her as if he thought she must be mad. Skittle refused to show any weakness to him and just pushed past him to the food bowls.

I love both my cats; they each have a role to fill in my life. One is the homebody, always nearby and the other provides the entertainment.

Strangle
Ricky, 28

My cat is a barn cat that my girlfriend picked up as a kitten. He is fond of sitting so high up on your chest that he's almost garrotting you so we called him Strangle. He is now about two years old, and weighs nearly fifteen pounds, which is mostly made up of muscle, not fat.

Strangle uses people as a scratching post. No matter how many times we get them from the vet he tries to scratch people's legs instead. Actually he has a long list of weird bits of behaviour.

Sometimes, he stretches his full length from the floor to the table to try and knock things off the table. He also acts as if he is supervising us. If my girlfriend and I sit together he sits in between us. When we go to bed and sit reading at night, he gets in between us, although we do evict him when we decide to turn the lights out.

Strangle has also terrified our dog Sal; if Sal forgets his place Strangle is always ready with claws and teeth to remind him where he sits in the pecking order. If I shout "Strangle" and open my arms wide he races up to me and leaps into my arms. He also begs for chocolate and goes for the postman if he's in the garden when the mail turns up.

All in all he's a little nutcase but he's also so cute and loving that we could never get rid of him no matter how much of a nuisance he makes himself.

Attacked by a Dog
Tasha, 35

One night last year, I was watching TV when I heard a loud commotion coming from my back garden. I went outside to find a strange man in my garden holding down a greyhound. The dog had attacked my cat Pinkie and there was blood everywhere. The owner had raced round the side of my house when his dog had escaped from his own yard and had managed to pull it off my cat.

Pinkie was on the other side of the garden and she was clearly scared and hurt. I immediately ran to pick her up. Her leg was covered in blood and badly deformed. As carefully as I could, I wrapped her in a soft towel and rushed to the emergency vet's surgery. I could tell she was in a lot of pain.

The vet told me that Pinkie's leg was fractured in numerous places and that our only option was to have the leg amputated. The operation cost a lot of money and I was worried how Pinkie would be afterwards but she seemed OK. We took her home with a lot of pain medication that, for once, she didn't seem to mind taking. After about six weeks she was back to her normal naughty self. She can jump onto windowsills and attack furniture even though she is missing a leg.

Water Cat
Hailey, 54

We have a lake at the bottom of our garden and each year some feral ducks visit us to show off their new ducklings, all tiny balls of yellow, brown, and cream fluff. They follow their mothers around in close formation, like a miniature convoy. Our cats Jimmy and Bobby are fascinated by these ducklings every year. Jimmy in particular will lie for hours among the long grass on the edge of the lake working out how to get one of these little birds for his breakfast. My son, Carl, tends to keep an eye out for him and usually scares the ducklings away if they try to come into our garden when either of the cats is out playing at hunting.

One morning, Jimmy ventured out onto the small wooden ramp that goes down into the lake, and lay there for about half an hour watching the ducks swimming and feeding just a few feet away from him. Finally, one duck attempted to get onto the garden shore and Jimmy could contain himself no longer. He flung himself into the air but as he did so Carl shouted at him. The end result was that Jimmy landed in the lake with a big splash. He gave out a yowl and went under the water but thankfully he re-surfaced very quickly. Carl was ready to dive into the lake to rescue him but even though he'd never done it before, Jimmy quite easily managed to swim to the bank where Carl gently lifted him out. We took him inside and wrapped him in a blanket because he'd started to shiver and we thought that maybe he was suffering from shock. It wasn't long before he was OK again. He gave up chasing ducklings that day and now just watches them sleepily from the garden

Obsessed with Birds…
Jill, 19

My cat Kizzy is obsessed with chasing birds. Every morning I am woken at dawn by Kizzy hurling herself at my bedroom window. I put the covers over my head and try to sleep but the yakking noise she makes and the thud of her body against the glass makes it very hard to go back to sleep.

If I stick my head out from under the covers, all I can see is her little head bobbing up and down. Now and then her whole body flies up the window attempting to attack the birds on the other side.

I honestly think the birds tease my cat on purpose. They know exactly what reaction they're going to get and at the same time they know that they're safe. Kizzy can't actually get them.

She always seems smart and elegant until she gets going after birds outside the window. Then she just seems a little bit ridiculous.

Pretty, Rascal and Tom
Jane, 30

I was never a cat lover until a few years ago. I had a dog and that seemed to be enough. Then we got our first cat, a grey tabby who we called Rascal. He was adorable and I realised that I was indeed a cat lover. I would take my dog, Scot, for a walk and Rascal would come along with us every day. If we stopped, he stopped. If we walked, he walked right along with us. This went on all summer. When the weather got cold Rascal would curl up on our sofa. When I took the dog out in the winter mornings he would remain on the sofa, he clearly thought that going outside in that sort of weather was foolish. He was always happy to see us when we returned and he and our dog get on surprisingly well together.

About a year later a friend of mine was asking around to see if someone would take in her mother's cat because her mother had to go into a nursing home. She has three greyhounds and didn't think they would take to having a cat in the house. So, then we got our second cat, Pretty. She is pure white with green eyes and she's really dainty and agile. Pretty and Rascal get on well and Pretty loves to start play fights by making a squeaky noise to Rascal and then lying on her back so that he jumps on her. Rascal gives her such a slap with his paws but she seems to love it.

Then we got our third cat, Tom, after I found him in an old barn while taking the dog and Rascal for a walk several years later. Tom was a small kitten, cold, hungry, thirsty and scared. He seemed to have been left to fend for himself. Anyway, when we got home I got the cat carry cage out and went back to get him. He didn't mind when I picked him up and put him in the cage. He meowed a bit on the way home but as soon as I let him out in the kitchen and showed him some food, he ran to the bowl and ate all the food in it without stopping to breathe.

Although Tom gets on with Rascal and Pretty, the animal he seems closest to is Scot. They often sleep together in Scot's dog basket and he seems quite protective of his little feline friend. Tom likes to sit on the back of the sofa and pat us on the shoulder when he wants something.

All my animals are special and it's lovely to live with so many of them.

Top Cats

In the wild, cats live in hierarchical groups, and some domestic cats still like to think that they are the ones who are in charge. One cat in the house often decides it is their job to order the food, to shout the house awake in the morning, or to see off unwanted visitors, including postmen and dogs!

Gogo
Nancy, 30

I have four cats but the strangest one is Gogo. Everyone thinks that he looks weird (some even say evil) and they are a little afraid of his pointy face and bright eyes, but to me he's an absolute darling. He has no sense of humour especially if he does something stupid like try to jump onto the dresser and miss, sliding down the front of it onto the floor. He just sits there afterward looking really pompous and grumpy because he knows he looked foolish.

He also likes to keep my other cats in check. They get a swift slap with a paw if they're being too interfering so they are prone to keep out of his way. When we have visitors, he growls at them if they sit in his favourite chair and he sounds like a goose when he eats. He also has the loudest yawn of any cat I've ever met. I just love him to bits.

Bossy Big Boy
Sally, 35

I have a cat called "Big Boy". He's an oriental shorthair and is very vocal and bossy. There is a chair in our sitting room that he has decided is his and his alone. We don't usually use it because you can't see the TV if you sit there. Last Christmas however, I invited the whole family round for Christmas dinner so there were quite a lot of us and of course someone had to sit in Big Boy's chair. My sister's husband Tom sat in the chair and immediately Big Boy was in front of him making loud insistent noises.

Tom didn't know Big Boy very well and remarked how communicative he was. Before I could explain, Big Boy jumped onto the back of his chair and began to chew the back of Tom's head. Tom tried to push him off but Big Boy then jumped from the back of his head to his lap where he continued biting Tom's knees. We were all helpless with laughter as Big Boy spent at least half an hour moving from one bit of Tom to the other giving him sharp little nips along the way. Big Boy had got so worked up that now even if Tom tried to get out of the chair, Big Boy would pounce on him and give him a little bite. Eventually Tom asked me to remove the cat so that he could get up.

When I lifted Big Boy off Tom Big Boy gave a warning yowl and glared at Tom. Tom got off the chair and eventually sat on the floor. Big Boy climbed back on his chair, gave a loud Mah noise and looked around the room as if he was looking to challenge anyone else who wanted to take him on in the fight for his favourite chair. No one volunteered so Big Boy yawned and then settled down to sleep. Tom remained on the floor all evening.

Scooter and Titch
Jeff, 56

I have two cats, both are boys, one is a big black and white cat called Scooter and the other is a much smaller part-tabby, part-oriental shorthair and we call him Titch. Though Titch the tabby is much smaller than Scooter, he is definitely the more dominant of the two and also the most jealous.

I recently had to go into hospital and ended up being there for five days and the whole time I was worrying about my cats. When I got home after the five days the hall carpet was covered in black and white fur. Scooter didn't want to leave my side so Titch sat on me every opportunity he had just to show Scooter who was boss. Scooter meowed and pushed against me, whilst Titch was quite disdainful of my absence as if to say "We managed quite well without you". At bedtime however, there was a different scenario. Titch was determined to snuggle up beside me in bed while Scooter sat on the other side of me, looking at me with his big green eyes and occasionally pawing my arm hopefully.

I adore both my cats and always try to please them both. If I don't, they head for the bathroom and rip up my toilet roll. It's nice to feel loved and wanted by your pets but sometimes I feel as if I'm their servant, here just to take care of their needs. I don't mind though. Once they've both settled themselves down we all go to sleep in a big warn purring pile.

Maisy the Troublesome Cat
Tracy, 25

I got my cat Maisy when she was a very tiny kitten and I had to hand feed her for about three weeks. The problem is that I think I spoiled her too much when she was a kitten because now she is a real trouble causer.

It's hard for me to get a full night's sleep because she does things that wake me up. She'll howl on the landing outside my bedroom door at 2am. If I've shut the bedroom door, she'll scratch on it or throw her body at it to make repeated thudding noises. If I shut her out she stands underneath the bedroom window, howling all night.

If I don't give her what she wants (her favourite cat food or her favourite jumper to sleep on), she'll charge at me and bite me.

If you walk by her she reaches out with her paw to grab your legs. She also hates me working and will repeatedly sit in front of my computer monitor or walk all over the keyboard. Mostly she loves to be stroked but then one time out of ten she'll lash out at you with her claws. It can be a bit unnerving, especially if you are not used to it. Most of the time she really is just a sweet little thing, but she really does believe she is entitled to have everything just the way she wants it.

Ebony
Ella, 43

We adopted a cat on Christmas Eve 1998. She was a sweet little black cat and we called her Ebony.

When they took her out of her cage and put her on a table, she looked at me and then rubbed her nose on me. I knew she was the cat for me. When we got her home she sat in front of the refrigerator when I opened it as if to say "I know this is where the best food is so get it out for me now!" She was so little but she had enormous ears and quite a bossy manner about her. She was always the one who was in charge.

Ebony was a very talkative cat. If you spoke to her she would always give you a reply. You always knew just how she was feeling by listening to her meows and watching her body language. We really spoiled her.

As she got older Ebony developed hyperthyroidism and had to take medicine for it. She was always good about taking medicine and for a while she was fine again. However in 2009 she began to get ill again. Her weight dropped dramatically and I could tell that she wouldn't be with us much longer.

We took her to the vet and she told us that Ebony was dehydrated and gave us an IV to take home and a bag of saline solution. At home I gently placed her in her basket and put a warm blanket over her. I was considering asking the vet to put her to sleep to stop her suffering because she was so weak, but we agreed to see how that night went.

Ebony never made it back to the vet, when I woke up the next morning she had died. I miss her so much. But if she had to go, I am glad she died in peace at home rather than in a vet's surgery. I buried her under her favourite 'bird-watching' bush in the garden and think about her often.

Jinx
Isobel, 40

My cat Jinx is a bit of a trouble-maker and fighter. At least once a week he comes home looking a bit worse for wear but very proud. You can tell he wins his fights. He even goes for our biggest dog Bruno. Bruno is a huge Rottweiler but Jinx still sits in front of him staring in a menacing manner. Sometimes, he gets into Bruno's basket, a place where no cat has ever dared to go. Bruno just sits there looking bewildered. Luckily he is not a mean dog, even though he looks scary to strangers.

If we give any table scraps to the dog, Jinx is in there grabbing it before Bruno can. He then tries to get Bruno to sniff his whiskers, so that the dog can tell how delicious his bit of food was, before sauntering off at a smug pace.

My husband loves him because he keeps mice away and can even catch birds by simply leaping into the air. He climbs up to our balcony to sneak into our bedroom. Sometimes I imagine him wandering the neighbourhood like some sort of gangster, provoking all the other cats to see who's in charge. Of course, he always wins.

Tiger
Carol, 49

I used to volunteer at a local cat rescue centre and one day someone brought in a little kitten they had found. I immediately fell in love with him and wanted to take him home. He was ginger and stripy and I called him Tiger.

Even though he was really tiny he strutted about as if he was the most powerful cat in the world. He had a very pompous expression on his face. When he attempted to wash and fell over instead, he got up and looked around as if he was daring anyone to laugh.

At home, Tiger quickly found his way around and then just sat in the kitchen and shouted for food. It's the first thing he does every morning. He doesn't meow hopefully like cats I've known before do, he just sits solidly on the floor and demands food with a deep "NOW" noise. Every visitor is inspected and either deemed suitable for the house (he gets on their laps and entertains them), or unsuitable (they get their ankles bitten).

He really does seem to think that he rules the roost. He's fully grown now and he's not an especially big cat, he's just a very confident one. Some of my friends are a bit scared of him and his judgmental temperament, but he's really a sweetie.

Cats and Children

Children and cats often get along very well, so long as the children know how to behave around animals. In this section we have stories about favourite pets and new additions to the house, and about how children get along with their pets and learn from them.

Alfie
Hank, 31 and Millie, 9

Alfie is very much my daughter's cat.

We got two kittens together, a male tabby and a white female kitten. When we went to see them, my daughter Millie, who was four at the time, immediately fell in love with the female kitten and called her Princess. She wasn't that interested in the tabby, who we called Alfie.

She spent the first couple of days trying to play with Princess, showing her Barbie dolls and sparkly fairy wands and so on. She was quite disappointed that Princess wasn't at all interested and tended to hiss and run away. (She is quite a temperamental cat even now she has grown up).

Millie soon switched her allegiance to Alfie once she realised how much more friendly he is. He was happy to be picked up and carried around. He even let he put little hats on him and dress him up. One time we went into her room and found her pushing him along on a little Barbie fairy carriage. He looked a bit confused but happy enough to just sit there.

You would have thought he'd have been scared or annoyed at all the attention she gave him but in fact he adored her from the start. One time after a week or so, she fell asleep on her side on the sofa, sucking her thumb, and he crept up to sit right on the side of her head and sat there purring. We have the picture of that on the kitchen wall and it makes me laugh still.

Eventually he grew up from being a kitten to being a cat, but he went right on letting her treat him as though he was her teddy bear. She would carry him around, make him do little dances and curl up holding him tight when she wanted comforting. Princess always seemed to treat him with disdain for being such a silly pet, but actually he gets a good deal out of it. She always gives him treats, he always has a warm lap to sit on.

He did stop sitting on her head, thankfully. But he can't be stopped from sleeping on her bed. The best I've managed to do is get her to accept that he sleeps at the bottom of the bed. We tried closing him out a few times, but either she snuck out of bed to open the door and let him in, or he howled the house down until we gave in for the peace.

To be honest, I wish I'd had a cat that was as affectionate as Alfie when I was a kid. It's really sweet that they are so close and even now she is nine she sees him as being her most special pet.

Once at school her teacher asked her who her role model was. She said "Alfie". But then when the teacher said it had to be a person, not a cat, she changed her mind and said it was her dad.

So at least I got second place!

Stringy
Harriet, 9

My cat Stringy eats cardboard boxes and she tries to eat plastic bags too! Now my dad is cross because she has started chewing the Christmas tree.

Drawing in Chalk
David, 31

When I was a little boy we usually used to go on holiday to the coast and stay in a caravan but I remember one year we went camping in a tent in the middle of the countryside. I remember that we were near some old castle that didn't interest me at all. I much preferred to go looking in rock pools. I was being a bit sulky so my mum said that I could go and explore the neighbouring field whilst her and my dad made some food on our camp fire.

I wandered along the path that ran along the edge of the field where there was a really tall crop growing. I didn't know what it was. But it looked like it would be fun to run and hide inside it so I began to head off into the middle of the field.

I hadn't got very far when I began to hear a sort of swishy rustling noise behind me. I couldn't see anything but it felt as if something very large was following me. In my child's imagination it was a tiger or a lion and I had to defeat it. I stopped in my tracks and listened but instead of a roar I heard a tiny little meow. I re-traced my steps and looked close to the ground. Eventually I saw a tiny white kitten. She re-started her meows as soon as she saw me as if she had decided that I was the one that had come to help her. I picked her up gently to take her back to our camp.

I had always wanted a puppy but had been told that I could not have one as I would not be able look after it, take it for walks and keep up with my school work. As I carried the kitten it came to me that my parents would not be able to put up as many objections to a cat as they had done to a dog. Perhaps this was my chance to have a pet of my own. The kitten however, struggled against being held and it got to the point where I couldn't really keep carrying her. Eventually I put her on the ground and kissed her goodbye. It seemed as if I had lost my chance to have an animal friend.

Reluctantly I set off for the campsite but then heard the rustling sound behind me again. I looked back and the kitten was following me. She followed me all the way to our tent. I went up to my mum who was setting out dishes on the fold-away table. I had been gone a long time and they weren't that happy with me so I didn't ask about taking the kitten home straight away, I just pretended that I was content to have her sit by me whilst I ate. I suggested that the kitten could get in the tent with me but was firmly told no so I left her outside and went to bed.

The next morning when I woke up, dad was already awake and I could hear him talking to someone quietly. I poked my head out of the tent and he was talking to the kitten and feeding her bits of sausage. He had already fallen for her. She played with us that day and the next day we were due to go home. I begged my mum and dad to let me keep the kitten and they said that I could but we had to find out if it belonged to anyone else first.

We packed up our stuff and dad drove us round to the farmer's house so we could pay him for the campsite. Dad mentioned the kitten and the farmer said that she was one of a litter of farm cats that had been born that summer and we were welcome to keep her if we wanted to. I called her Chalk and she was my pet for the next fifteen years.

A Cat and a Baby
Jo, 29

I got Shelby when he was three months old, from an advertisement in the window of my local grocery shop. I've had him four years now and I was pregnant when I got him. I desperately wanted something to cuddle and look after. I think it was my mind wanting something to practice mother-skills on. My husband was sceptical at first, thinking that it would be a bad plan to have a cat when the baby arrived, but eventually he relented and I got Shelby.

Shelby took to being mothered very easily and he was actually fine when my daughter was born. I worried that there might be some jealousy but there really wasn't. He just calmly walked into the room and gave her a good sniff, and then he walked around her cot. Then she started to cry and he jumped back in alarm. I think he hadn't realised she was alive. He also didn't like her crying but then crying babies are never the favourite sound of anyone. But he got used to the idea and was never any trouble with her.

My daughter is now running around and her favourite pastime is 'chase the cat'. Shelby has his little hiding places however, where he can sleep undisturbed and everything is working out fine.

Snuggle
Sara, 10

My cat Snuggle always sleeps on my bed with me and makes me feel safe. When he is with me I can sleep facing the wall but if he's not in the room I need to face the door so that I can see if anyone comes in. He is very fluffy because he is a Persian cat and my mum complains that he leaves hair everywhere but I don't mind. He likes me to brush him and then there is hair everywhere.

Allergic to Cats
Connor, 19

As a child I was frequently ill and between the ages of about seven and nine I spent a lot of time at home because I was too ill to go to school. I had all the symptoms of asthma but all the tests showed that I didn't have that condition. The doctors were puzzled and I saw various specialists but no one had any answers.

On the days that I was at home, our cat Sissy used to keep me company. She would curl up beside me as I watched TV and I would scratch her behind the ears. All the time my breathing was raspy and I felt quite weak. The mystery was solved by a family visitor who suggested that I was possibly allergic to cats.

I had tests at the hospital and our visitor was right. It was our cat that was affecting my breathing and my energy. We all loved the cat though and couldn't get rid of her. My parents re-decorated my bedroom and put in a new carpet and my room became a no-go area for Sissy.

She died when I was eleven and I missed her badly but instead of getting another cat we got a puppy so that I could play with it without getting ill. I still like cats a lot, but these days I have to stick to watching cute videos of them on the internet.

The Wandering Feline

In this section we have included stories about cats who are wanderers, from strays, holiday visitors and passers-by to cats who come to stay, or who take it on themselves to move in with a new household.

December Present
Jen, 62

I have to tell you about how I got my first cat, back in the 1980s. I was coming home from work late one December evening. It was already dark and I was looking forward to getting myself some food, putting my feet up and watching TV before going to bed. I was working in a hospital at the time and it was very understaffed so I was always very tired when I got home from my shift.

As I got near to my front door I heard a tiny squeaking noise coming from my lavender plants under my front window. It was very dark so I couldn't see what it could be. My first thoughts were that it might be an injured rat or something similar and I didn't really want to look but I work in the nursing profession and I can't leave anything in pain no matter what sort of animal it is.

I went inside, took the torch that I keep in the kitchen and went back outside to investigate. I crouched down and looked underneath the bushes and I saw that the noise was being made by a tiny kitten. It couldn't have been more than a few weeks old. It was tiny and a light grey colour with darker grey stripes running along its body and tail. As gently as I could I picked up the little kitten and took it inside.

Once inside I took it into the kitchen to get a good look at it. It was squeaking loudly and was definitely hungry. I put a little milk onto a teaspoon and put the spoon against the kitten's face. It began to drink greedily. I'd never had a cat before and so didn't really know what to do with it; I didn't even know if it was a boy or a girl. The husband of one of my friends is a vet so I decided to give her a call to see if he could come over and have a look at it.

Daniel turned up about half an hour later and came into the kitchen to investigate what I'd found. He concluded that it was a male kitten about four weeks old and warned me that looking after it at this age would be hard work. I'd have to feed it every few hours, day or night, and keep its face and body clean with moistened cotton wool balls. He offered to take it with him and try to find someone who could adopt it through various cats' charities that he knew from his veterinary surgery.

I don't know what came over me at the time but I'm sure that the kitten gave another squeak and gazed straight at me. I felt compelled to look after the little creature and said so to Daniel. He looked at me as if I was mad. He said that I would have to feed it several times a day and night for at least six weeks. I said I didn't mind, I had at least three weeks annual leave owing to me and I was happy to use it to take care of this kitten. Daniel agreed to go to his surgery and get me some syringes and special kitten milk. While he was gone I found an old angora sweater upstairs that I hadn't worn for years and brought it down to make a little bed for my new lodger. I called him Herby because of where I'd found him.

The first few days were very hard. Herby needed a lot of attention. Even when he wasn't feeding he seemed to need to be close to me so that he wouldn't feel lost and all alone again. I turned my angora sweater into a sling and carried him with me whenever I had things to do.

As he grew, Herby became more and more adventurous. He often got into my handbag and dragged items out of it around the floor. He climbed up a leather jacket that I had hanging on the back of the kitchen door, making lots of little scratch marks in the leather. I remember the day I gave him some cream for the first time, he climbed up the curtains and glared around the room with large dark eyes. Even though he could be a nuisance I knew that I could never be without him. He was so playful. When I changed the bedding on my bed he pounced onto the sheets as I was pulling them off. When I took my laundry out of the laundry box he dived into the middle of it. There was never a dull moment.

Eventually I went back to work and when I returned home Herby was always waiting for me behind the door. As soon as he saw me come in he would turn around and head straight to the kitchen so that I would be in no doubt that he wanted some food. After dinner he would curl up with me on the sofa and watch TV until bedtime when we would both head upstairs to bed. I would get under the covers and he would snuggle down on top of them.

Herby lived with me until his death seventeen years later. I think we had an extra special bond because he'd been hand reared by me. He died peacefully in his sleep but I was devastated by losing him. It was a year before I could even contemplate getting another cat. I did eventually get another one but Herby still holds a very special place in my memories.

Coming Home
Lena, 37

Many years ago I took in a black kitten with a little white spot on his back that I called Spot. A few years later when I split up with my husband, I moved with my daughter to a small one bedroom apartment where I couldn't keep Spot with me. I was devastated but there was nothing for it and so I gave him up for adoption to the local animal shelter.

For many years I wondered about my little cat, hoping that he was happy and doing OK. When my daughter was ten I started volunteer work at the animal charity, playing with the cats to keep them used to humans. One day we had a new arrival and I could see that it was a large black cat. He had been living with an old lady who had been taken into a nursing home, so her friend had brought her back to the place where he had come from.

When he turned around I saw the white spot on his back and I knew it was my cat Spot. I'm sure he recognised me too, as he kept pushing his head against me and purring when I kissed the top of his head. I now live in a bigger house with my new partner, so I decided to take him home with me and my family. It is so wonderful that he has come back to me.

Clara
Lara, 29

My first cat was called Clara and she was the best kind of cat you could have. She was a rescue cat. She was found in a bedraggled, exhausted state on the edge of a lake behind someone's house. She must have fallen in somewhere, but they couldn't track down the owners.

Ever since I've had her, she has refused to go anywhere near water. The first time she saw me in the bath she stood at the bathroom door and screeched at me, getting very agitated. Because she couldn't get me out she went all over the house giving a plaintive meow that sounded like a cry for help. I think she wanted someone to come and get me out of the bath. When I got out to dry myself, she purred and rubbed around my ankles with relief. To this day I can only have a bath with the door shut and even then she sits outside giving me a little meow now and again which I have to answer to show her that I'm OK.

Duster
Lily, 24

I used to have a little black cat called Duster who ran away once. I was so upset because I was sure that I'd never see him again. I thought that he had probably got lost. However, he actually came home after four days looking hungry and scared. After I let him in he meowed all night and wouldn't leave my side. All evening he climbed over me, rubbing his ears against me and giving me his gentle little head butts under my chin. He was clearly pleased to be back at home.

Ever since then he always has to be near to me. He hugs me every morning by putting his paws around my neck and when I cuddle him back he goes into what I called his crazy mood and charges around the house jumping all over the furniture. Then he lies down on my rug and pulls himself across it slug-like using his claws, which means I have to tell him off a bit too.

Last week I was waiting at the bus stop up the road when I realised that Duster had followed me. I had to take him back home because he would probably have got on the bus with me. Still, I love him dearly.

Stray under the Bed
Sophie, 32

A long time ago we got two kittens, one male and one female. A friend had found them in an abandoned playground and we agreed to take them in.

We decided to allow the female cat to have a litter of kittens before having her spayed and of course once she came into season, our back garden was full of a motley collection of tomcats. We even gave them nicknames, Grey Tom, Hobo Tom, Tiny Tom, and so on. It was spring and the kitchen door was always left open to air the house. The cats fought at night and our female cat Stella was always out tormenting them.

We kept our bedroom door closed at night because both cats were a nuisance in the bedroom. They climbed on top of things and jumped on you so we took the decision to ban them.

A few days after Stella finished being in season we started to notice a strange smell in the bedroom. It smelled of tomcat. We kept thinking that one of the cats must have got in but they were both in the living room so it wasn't them.

After a couple of days with the smell getting worse and worse we decided to completely search every nook and cranny of the bedroom. It was then that we found Hobo Tom under our bed. He must have sneaked into the bedroom at some point during the daytime, become trapped and panicked.

He was an extremely aggressive feral cat and all attempts to get him out from under the bed resulted in ferocious growling. Eventually my husband pushed him out from the other side with a broom and Hobo Tom ran into the hall. He then cowered in a corner still growling until my husband appeared with the broom again and shunted him into the kitchen and out of the door.

We actually had a tomcat under our bed for two days and didn't find him. He must even have been there when whilst we were asleep. It's always a good story to tell people. How we didn't notice him before we will never know.

The Secret Cats
Tim, 37

I found my cats Charlie and Archie in a box behind the retail park car park when I was working nights as a security guard. As I came off duty I saw a cardboard box by the fence and when I went over to investigate I found two tiny black and white kittens staring up at me. Someone must have left them there overnight. It was a chilly dawn and I didn't want to leave them there so I picked up the box, put it in my car and took it home.

At the time, me and my wife, who was then my girlfriend, lived in a rented house. We weren't supposed to have pets but we decided that we would keep them and hide them from the landlord. The kittens were so much fun, running in and out of cupboards and behind the cooker. I remember one time we had to get the landlord round to have a look at the boiler and we had to put the cats into a box and take them round to a nearby friend's house. We hid all the cat paraphernalia and the landlord was never the wiser. We got away with having secret cats, although I remember my wife having to sew up the hem in the curtains where the kittens had made themselves a hammock. We didn't have much money in those days and often the cats ate better than we did.

Eventually we got a more permanent place to live where we could openly have cats and things were much easier. They've been with us twelve years now and they are very much part of our little family. It's strange how they have been so much part of our lives after that first morning in the car park. It's hard to remember what our lives were like before we had cats.

Kitten Stories

This section includes stories about young cats and kittens and how they adapted to their new homes.

Hello Kitty
Mary, 43

I was always more of a dog person than a cat person. But I was won over by a tiny scrap of a thing that came to live in my home some years ago.

I was at a friend's house with my daughter who was then five years old when my friend's brother turned up with a tiny grey tabby kitten in his hands. He went straight to my daughter and put the kitten into her lap. I could see from the look on my daughter's face that there was no way I would be able to separate her from the tiny purring animal in her hands, so I agreed that we could take it home. My friend's brother told me that he had found the kitten behind some bushes in his garden and because he has two large, fierce dogs he couldn't keep it but wanted to find it a good home.

As I tucked my daughter into bed with the kitten sitting next to her, we talked about what to call her. At the time she was a huge fan of Hello Kitty... so the kitten's name became Kitty.

Kitty bonded with our little family quickly and proved to have an excellent nature with my daughter and her friends. They used to dress her up and push her around in the dolls pram but she never scratched or bit them. If she'd had enough she would simply go outside for a bit. If I thought their games were becoming too much for Kitty I would tell them to leave her alone. Kitty had a method to end the playing; she would give me a certain look that said, "Tell them to leave me alone", and I would.

Within the year of Kitty coming to live with us, I had another child and she grew to love crawling after Kitty who jumped all over the furniture to avoid (and unwittingly entertain), her. However, one day my youngest had got Kitty backed into a corner and was pushing her luck trying to grab at the cat. The cat gave me the look and I told my youngest daughter to leave Kitty alone. My daughter ignored me and Kitty made a threatening noise, like a low growl and aimed a hiss at her face. Immediately my daughter let go of the cat and began crying because the cat had behaved meanly to her. I explained that whilst cats like to play, when they give out signals that they don't want to play or are clearly trying to get away then we should leave them be. Every time the girls behaved like that with her, we would repeat the routine and on cue every time she would growl but never scratch or bite.

In the mornings, when the alarm went off, Kitty would come in and wake me up by touching my nose with her paw and then follow me to the girls' room to help me wake them up. (They also got their noses pawed). Kitty would jump up to the window sill to watch them set off for school. If they were outside in the garden, she stuck to them like a little bodyguard and watched them closely. She always alerted me with a meow when she thought they were too far from the house. As the girls got older I had to reassure her they were just going for a walk and it was OK for them to go now because they were big girls. Still she would wait for them, watching out for them until they came back.

Kitty had a few litters of kittens in her time and proved to be an excellent little mother. I cleaned out a dresser drawer for her and put in some old sweaters to make it comfy and that's what she used for her "nest". She kept the kittens in it until they were old enough to wander. I was there for every birth, she would not deliver unless I was there, talking quietly to soothe her. If I tried to leave the room she would attempt to follow me even in advanced labour. After the third litter I had her spayed because I was worried that so many litters might be difficult for her. Most cats will hide and protect their kittens but Kitty allowed us to come and have a look at them. Of course, I would never allow the girls to hurt the kittens and we left her alone to raise them as she wished.

Even though she was open and gentle with us, she was a good hunter. The mice and rats never lasted long near our house. She used to come in with a special meow that meant she had caught something. At night she would just leave these dead animals outside my bedroom door like presents. I remember one time, being in the kitchen cooking the supper, when Kitty came charging through the cat door with a little bird fluttering in her mouth. I chased her back out through the cat door and so she got rid of it.

When my brother and his wife came to visit they brought their two sheepdogs with them. Through the whole visit Kitty would get them to chase her and then look on smugly as they got told off for breaking things and knocking things over as they chased her. They could never catch her because she was too agile and familiar with our kitchen.

Every visitor we have ever had fell in love with Kitty. She has always been a people cat; she's loved them, purred for them and greeted them at the door. She's always loved to be stroked and given lots of attention. Lately her age is showing and she has slowed down quite a bit but her lively spirit is still there in her eyes. I do worry about losing her; she has been such a central force in our family. My daughters are now both teenagers and she has been the only pet they've ever known. We're determined to savour every day we have left with her.

The Right Place at the Right Time
Hannah, 60

When I was a little girl I desperately wanted a pet cat. My mum was always reluctant to get one because she worried about it scratching the furniture. Eventually she said that if a kitten came to me I could keep it but otherwise I should shut up about it because she wasn't going to look for a cat for me. At the time we lived on the fourth floor a block of flats so I didn't have a garden where I could leave out saucers of milk to lure cats to me. I actually felt very sad because I knew it was mum's way of saying "no cat".

A few weeks later I was walking down the stairs when I heard a tiny high pitched squeak. I looked around and on a small ledge behind the railings was a kitten! I carefully leant forward and picked it up. It was very tiny, grey and stripy and had round blue eyes that stared at me. As quickly as I could I ran back to our flat and showed mum that a kitten had finally come to me. She was suspicious as to where I'd got him from and insisted that we put some "lost kitten" posters up around the neighbourhood, but did agree that I could keep him if no one else claimed him. I had already secretly called him Lucky and prayed that he would be allowed to live with us.

After about two days someone actually contacted us about the kitten. I was holding my breath as Mum talked on the phone but as she put the receiver down she was smiling. Apparently the kitten had been part of a litter of four and had somehow escaped from the kitchen where they lived. The woman who phoned said that she had been trying to find homes for all the kittens anyway and that if we wanted to we could keep Lucky. Mum told me later that evening that she had become very fond of him and was very happy that he could stay with us.

Lily
Cathy, 22

I have a lovely kitten called Lily. She's a very easy kitten to take care of and I can already tell that she's a creature of habit. She gets up when I get up and eats her breakfast as I sit at the kitchen table eating mine. I have an exercise bike that I like to use after breakfast and at the same time Lily goes running around the house, getting her own form of exercise. When I sit down at my computer, Lily comes and sits on the edge of my desk.

In the evenings when I watch TV, Lily curls up with me on the sofa. I'm so glad that I brought her home.

The Garden Kittens
Samantha, 48

A few years ago, I found a litter of kittens in our back garden. They had somehow got into our garden shed, their mother was with them and she was clearly a stray. I didn't want to disturb them but I decided to help by bringing the mum some tuna and water every day. I started to look forward to seeing the tiny kittens each day as I took out the water and food. As the mother began to trust me she brought her kittens out into the garden to play. One afternoon, I watched them scampering around the garden. There was a grey one, a black and white one, a black one, and a ginger and white stripy one. They all looked so sweet exploring the bushes and playing with each other.

One night there was a huge thunderstorm and I went out to the shed to make sure that they were OK. When I peered through the door I could see four tiny terrified faces looking back at me. Water had got into the shed and the floor was flooding. I just knew that I had to get them indoors. We got a large cardboard box and me and my husband gently put the kittens into it. The mother just watched and then placidly followed us all up to the house. I got them settled for the night in the kitchen and they seemed quite content to be warm and dry and I gave them and their mother some food and water.

I didn't really want cats, so, the next morning I telephoned the local animal shelter to see about taking them there. The woman at the shelter said that if no one rescued them they would be put to sleep and I didn't want that. Instead I phoned around my family and friends and secured homes for three of the kittens. Then I looked at them wandering around my kitchen poking their faces into all the corners

My daughter who was at college at the time, said she wanted to take one of the kittens home with her and she took the ginger one.

By then I had absolutely fallen in love with the grey one who seemed to have also become attached to me and followed me everywhere. A friend had said that she would take two, so we agreed that I could keep the grey one and she would take the black one and the black and white one. From having never had cats, I now ended up with two. The mother still has a bit of wanderlust about her and disappears for days at a time even though I have had her spayed. I've called her Missy. Every time she turns up she's very insistent that she needs food and then indulges in a bit of play fighting with her son. I've called the little grey boy kitten Smokey because of his lovely colour and he rarely ventures further than our garden hedge. He's happy on the sofa watching TV or on one of the beds sleeping.

The nice thing is that I get to see the other three kittens as well. My daughter called the ginger kitten Pippin and he's a really laidback sleepy cat. The black and white one is called Stella and she's outgoing and friendly. The black kitten is called Coco and she's as shy as her sister is bold.

I'm really happy that everything turned out well for them and have realised, quite late in life, that I am a cat person.

Sooty
Bethany, 31

I have a one-year-old white long-haired cat called Sooty. When he was a kitten he would wander around the house shouting and he was only happy when he was close enough to touch me. He even seemed to want me to go with him to his food bowl. I thought he was just being extra friendly and enjoyed being around me but when I took him to the vet for his six month check-up, the vet had some shocking news for me. Sooty was blind. Once I found that out a lot of his odd behaviour made sense. It hasn't changed the way I feel about him. If anything I am more protective of him. He loves being stroked and chatted to and we spend many happy hours together, in the garden in the summer or cosy and warm indoors during the winter. He is very cuddly and it's lovely to know that he trusts me so much.

Senior
Kate, 36

I have an orange stripy cat called Senior. I called him Senior because when I got him he always had a very pompous, serious little face and looked like an old cat in a tiny cat's body.

As a kitten, he used to sneak into the bathroom while I was having a soak. He would then stand on his hind legs and pat at the bubbles with his paw. Once, he leapt onto the edge of the tub for a closer look. He began to pat more bubbles and was clearly delighted with them because he began purring away.

He decided that he wanted to explore further, and stepped across the taps onto the other side, where the rim of the tub is much narrower. He had no space to turn, and it was wet and slippery. Suddenly, he slipped and slid down the side of the bath into the water. It was as if I was watching it in slow motion as his little face sunk beneath the bubbles. Yet, it happened so fast I couldn't prevent it.

I managed to grab him and pull him out of the water. He had a huge ball of bubbles on his head and I couldn't stop laughing even though he was clearly furious with the situation. He reacted as if I had lured him there so that I could try to drown him. I got out of the bath and wrapped us both in towels, then took him into the bedroom where I could get him properly dry. Eventually he returned to normal but whenever I get in the bath now he just comes in the bathroom and gives me a look that tells me how stupid he thinks I am with my game and he's not playing.

Minxie
Sue, 28

My cat's name is Minxie. She is only about four months old. She is a very playful and friendly young cat. She is never afraid to go up to new people and demand that they play with her by taking one of her toys over and dropping it in their lap. I have only had her for about a month, but I am already very attached to her. She keeps me very good company when my husband is away. She comes and sleeps in my lap, plays, and meows and follows me around. She's always doing something that makes me laugh such as sitting in the bathroom sink or hiding completely flat under the furniture so that it takes me ages to work out where she is.

I am so happy that I got her

Stuck up a Tree
Veronica, 25

My parents have a house in the country with a large garden and they have two old cats and half a dozen chickens. Last winter they decided to get another kitten when one of their friends had a litter that they needed to find homes for. The kitten was a little tabby cat called Tumble because he's always finding ridiculous situations to get involved with. From the beginning you would find him on top of the kitchen cupboards or the wardrobes and to get down he'd literally fling himself downwards periodically bouncing against the cupboard doors until he got to the floor. Tumble is a very loving kitten too. He loves to be held, cuddled and stroked and is very playful.

My mum had decided that Tumble shouldn't be allowed out of the house until spring, when he would be more used to his surroundings but he was having none of that. After about two weeks he made a run for it when my father was taking out the rubbish. Their drive has four tall poplar trees along it and he made straight for the nearest one and climbed up straight to the top. These trees are about twenty foot high and none of us could just reach up to get him down again.

We shouted his name but all that happened was the sound of his tiny, squeaky meow from the branches at the very top of the tree. You could see his little face poking out now and then but it was clear that he had no plan for bouncing down from such a height. My dad went to the garage to get out the decorating ladder but even fully extended it only reached half way up the tree. A few neighbours turned up to see what the commotion was all about. One of the neighbours brought a bigger ladder but even that didn't reach to the top of the tree and it was too dangerous for him to reach up and try to grab at Tumble as he scrabbled about at the top of the tree.

We eventually called the fire brigade and they weren't much use. They told us that there would be a delay because there was a large fire on a local industrial estate and all their crew were currently very busy, but they would try and come later if they could. By this time Tumble had been up the tree for about two hours and it was getting dark; the weather was also deteriorating and the wind was building up. As it got colder, poor Tumble began to meow louder and none of us had any idea what to do.

As we all stood there, a car came along the road and the driver slowed down when he saw the crowd of us standing there looking up at the tree. He asked us what the problem was and told us that he thought he could help. He worked for the local council, mending street lights and had access to a special vehicle with a controlled lift mechanism that you sat in to be lifted up to the height of a street light. He offered to go and get it and have a go at rescuing Tumble for us.

Half an hour later he had the council vehicle parked on the drive and one of his colleagues was in the bucket seat being lifted towards the top of the tree. When the man finally reached up to get hold of Tumble, the cat jumped gratefully into his arms and we all cheered as he was brought down. Tumble snuggled up to my mum when he was handed over and taken inside for some food and a drink. Everyone hoped that the experience would have taught him a lesson but he's still as much of a darcdevil as ever.

Freddy the Protective Cat
Anna, 38

I once rescued five small kittens from beneath my house. I already had a big male cat called Freddy when I took them in. I was worried that Freddy wouldn't take to the kittens, but he instantly fell in love with them. He seemed to want to be near them all the time and he became fiercely protective of them. It was as if they were his litter of kittens and he was the parent.

One day, one of the kittens developed a case of diarrhoea. His fur was covered in excrement and he smelled awful so I had to give him a bath. I filled my kitchen sink with some warm water and, using a little bit of soap, I began to wash the kitten very gently. While I was bathing the kitten it started to cry loudly. Then all of a sudden I felt something heavy bang into my leg. It was Freddy. He had jumped up at my leg and sunk his teeth into the back of my thigh. I dropped the kitten and shrieked. I was in shock. I couldn't believe that my own cat attacked me. I guess he heard the kitten crying and thought I was hurting it. No one was allowed to do any harm to those little kittens.

Once I got the kitten out of the sink and into a warm towel he calmed down and sat licking her all over. I don't think any mother cat could have been more caring that Freddy was with those kittens.

Dindins
Louis, 26

I am a typical 'cat person' and I shortly after I left college I adopted a kitten who I hoped would be living with me for a long time. A colleague had a kitten that she wanted to get rid of because it was scratching her furniture and since my home is like a tip anyway, I figured a kitten wouldn't really make things much worse. I really missed having cats as a student and seeing as I'd now moved into my own apartment, I decided that it was finally time for me to get my own.

I went over to my colleague's house and met the little chap who was going to come and live with me. He was the tiniest kitten with big blue eyes and black and white fur. I knew I'd made the right choice to agree to adopt him. He had a little white blob over his left eye that gave his face a quizzical expression, a very long tail and huge paws.

I picked him up and he set about clawing holes in my sweater then chewed on the knees of my jeans. He was clearly very playful and twitched his large ears and meowed at me as I introduced myself to him. I think he's actually a mixed breed because his large ears and long tail make him look a bit Siamese. I put him into the carry case I'd brought with me and drove home with him giving me squeaky meows as I tried to reassure him.

Back home I put him on the litter tray I'd bought thinking that it was important to make sure he knew where it was. He sat in it looking bewildered and then proceeded to kick the litter all over the kitchen floor. He then climbed onto the windowsill and began doing battle with the geraniums. I began to wonder why I had agreed to take in this creature. He clearly wasn't going to do what he was told. It was more like he'd decided to live with me but there were some things in my apartment that weren't to his liking, such as the litter tray and plants on windowsills.

This kitten knew no orders, or boundaries. He was adorable but in the days when he first came to live with me I had to make a lot of adjustments. The plants had to go from the windowsills and he seemed to want to go outside for his toilet so, as I fortunately live on the ground floor, I had a cat door put in leading out from the kitchen. He was so bouncy and interested in everything that I was often relieved when he curled up and went to sleep. The rest of the time he climbed, jumped and poked his face into everything he could. He tore almost everything I own to shreds and interrupted anything I tried to do. Then he'd curl up on my lap and purr loudly to let me know what fun he was having.

Naming him proved to be almost as difficult as owning him. I like to take time to name a cat because I think it should reflect their personality. For about a week I just said "Stop it!" to him and he'd look at me with glee then scamper off to do damage somewhere else. In the end I called him Dindins because that seemed to get his attention more than anything else. Whenever I shouted "Dindins" at him he would stop what he was doing and come over to pester me.

Dindins loved being outside. I loved to watch him through the window as he pounced on the plants, hid under bushes and stalked birds. He would chase bees and butterflies and leap up to try to catch them, sometimes falling on his face when he missed, making me laugh. Every day brought more fun from him and no matter how bad his behaviour or how much I admonished him for it, he spent every evening curled up with me on the sofa and all night sleeping on the end of my bed.

Unfortunately, Dindins tested positive for Feline Leukaemia Virus when he was five years old. The vet told me that he probably didn't have much time left. I felt so sad that all I could think to do was rush home, cuddle him, and try to assure him that everything was going to be OK.

Ever since I got this news, I try to spend more time with Dindins, hugging him, and trying to will good health into his body. Dindins seems totally oblivious to his condition, and for now remains in apparently good health. The vet said that he's not in any pain and he still seem to enjoy his food although not as much as he used to. When I return in the evenings he's always sitting by the door waiting for me. I dread the day when he won't be.

Button the Explorer
Tom, 23

I have just bought a little chocolate brown Burmese kitten and I've called her Button. As soon as I brought her home Button set about exploring the house. She poked her little face into every nook and cranny and then looked at me with a little expression that seemed like it was her way of telling me approved of her new abode.

I had to go outside to weed the garden and because she was so young and new to the house I left her shut in the kitchen so that she wouldn't get lost. She wasn't having that at all. She got onto the kitchen window sill and gave such a cacophony of high pitched mewlings that I had to go back inside a couple of times to calm her down.

I don't know how much longer I can keep her in the house when I'm in the garden. I might have to think up some sort of portable carrying vessel. She is so affectionate. She keeps going to sleep at the top of my head on the pillow. I think it's because the only bit of me she can see when I'm under the covers is my head and she wants to be close to me. Also, it's really hard for me to photograph her because she refuses to stay still and keeps coming over to investigate the camera. I've clearly bought myself a proper little madam.

My Cat Thinks He's a Puppy
Kim, 36

I bought my Oriental Shorthair about five years ago and drove a four hour round trip to collect him. He was an adorable kitten, jet black with green eyes and enormous ears. The woman I bought him from worked in a vet's practice and had quite a collection of animals. In the kitchen where the kittens were living there was also a large cage containing a black Staffordshire bull terrier female with a litter of black pups. The woman told us that our kitten, Jacques, spent most of his time playing with the puppies. She had been worried at first that the dogs might attack him but they had accepted him and were happy to share their space.

When we finally got Jacques home we realised that he had a lot of dog-like behaviour. When you picked him up he sniffed all over your face like a puppy would do. He also growled and ran to the door if somebody came to visit. He still doesn't sit down neatly like a cat; he leans sideways and then flops down. I think the puppies must have influenced his behaviour quite a lot. One of my friends came to visit and when she saw Jacques eating she said that he ate like a dog too. He wolfs it down in great gulps. He also bites when he's not happy with something.

He likes to follow you up and down the road as well. Sometimes it's a bit like having a cat-shaped dog.

Love Cat
Becky, 62

I went to the local animal shelter to get a kitten. When I got there and looked at the kittens, I fell in love with a tiny chocolate point Siamese. I was told they were all available except for the Siamese who was only five weeks old and had been given to the shelter by a couple who were going to live abroad and therefore, couldn't keep him. He hadn't been chosen for re-homing but I think one of the people who worked there had wanted him which was why he wasn't available. All the other cats were grown up and I really wanted a kitten so I didn't pick any cat at all that day. As I was leaving the building, the girl who had shown me the kittens followed me out. She asked if I would like the tiny Siamese. She told me that if I would wait she might be able to persuade her colleague to let me take him as she could see how disappointed I was that I couldn't have it. So, I waited for her, and fifteen minutes later she came and gave the kitten to me.

He was so tiny. I could tell right away there was something different about him. He bonded to me instantly and snuggled inside my jacket as soon as I got him home. He only tolerated other people by sniffing them and then walking away. He grew so quickly that at seven months he weighed ten pounds. I took him in to my local pet shop and they said that he was mixed with some other kind of cat; he wasn't a pure-breed Siamese which was why he had grown so much bigger than a typical Siamese.

He is such a fun cat. He tries to bury his food under the newspaper I put down under the cat dish and sticks his paws into any water he finds. He has long fur between the pads of his feet. He also does not purr loudly and is very territorial about my home. He has sometimes tried to attack strangers if they come into my house. He is very protective of me and rushes to the door whenever someone knocks. He greets me every morning when I wake up and stays in whatever room I am in. He is my great companion and gives me comfort and joy. I would be totally lost without him. He looks like a chocolate point Siamese but acts more like a guard dog.

Cats and their Nine Lives

Cats are well known for their escapades and misadventures. These are stories about cats that have risked life and limb but always seem to land on their feet.

Anniversary Celebrations
Minnie, 40

My husband and I decided to celebrate our anniversary with a bottle of sparkling wine. When he brought it back from the shop it was fairly warm so we decided to put it into the freezer to cool it faster. Unfortunately we forgot about it and by the time we remembered it looked on the verge of being frozen when we took it out of the freezer.

Our cat Bingo was in the kitchen eating his food peacefully when my husband attempted to pop open the wine. We hadn't thought about the consequences of opening a pressurised bottle of sparkling wine. The cork came out with a huge bang like a gunshot. After flying around the kitchen it hit Bingo behind his back legs. With a screech he leapt about four feet into the air. At the same time freezing droplets of sparkling wine tumbled down onto his head.

Bingo was covered in frozen wine and extremely upset about whatever it had been that hit him in the backside. He promptly fled the kitchen and headed upstairs.

When we found him he had taken refuge in our bed, under the duvet. Our sheets were soaked with sparkling wine and Bingo smelled like a brewery. I decided to change the sheets whilst my husband cleaned him up a bit. From the bedroom I could hear the howls of protest in the bathroom. I looked in to see a furious Bingo sitting in the sink, his fur sticking up in all directions. We brought him downstairs and put him on a towel by the radiator where he gradually dried out. To this day, every time we open a bottle of wine he runs from the room as fast as he can.

Road Runner
Jonathan, 32

About four years ago my wife and I were driving home after having dinner at a friend's house. Suddenly I saw something in my head-lights and automatically swerved to avoid it. I couldn't be sure whether I had hit it or not so I pulled over and got out of the car.

I walked over to it slowly because I didn't really want to see something that had been squashed onto the road. I could see it was some sort of animal about the size of a small rat. I bent down to inspect it and saw that it was a small grey kitten, which was just sitting there, shaking. Luckily I had managed to brake in time.

I touched it gently and it didn't seem to be hurt so I picked it up and carried it back to the car and showed to my wife. Just to be sure we took the kitten to our local emergency veterinarian clinic to get it checked over. The vet told us that it was a male kitten about 13 weeks old and, other than being a bit cold, seemed to be in good health.

We took him home and wrapped him in one of my old gardening sweaters to warm him up. Because of the way we found him, we called him Road Runner or Roadie for short and he is still with us. We have moved to a different area but he shows no sign of wanting to wander off. He wakes us up every morning by chirruping in our ears, and races us to the kitchen when we get out of bed. It really feels as if he was meant to be our cat and was just waiting for us that night.

Emma and Ernie
Claire, 29

My two cats are called Emma and Ernie, and they are both naughty in their own ways. Emma is a sweet, grey tabby girl who loves to have a cuddle. She is also very opinionated - always speaking her mind and leaving us in no doubt when she wants something. Emma spends her days finding new ways to show us her chubby belly, inviting us to give it a stroke. She's mastered the art of getting someone to pet her whenever she wants.

Emma loves to hide, believing nobody can see her, whether it is in a box, beneath a rug, or under the coffee table. She's funny in a sweet, loving way, but you would have to know her to really appreciate her good nature. Our cat Ernie is a different story!

Ernie is about two weeks younger than Emma and mainly black with white socks; they are not brother and sister. Both cats are now around eighteen months old but Ernie still thinks he is a kitten. He loves to jump and climb onto everything, from the refrigerator to the windowsill to the top of doors. He is a daredevil acrobat who can balance himself on the narrowest of ledges. There is nowhere in our home that he hasn't explored or sniffed, from the tops of bookcases to the cupboard under the bathroom sink.

As long as he stays off the kitchen work tops and dining room table, we pretty much let Ernie climb and jump anywhere he wants to. We're lucky that so far he's not broken any ornaments or valuables. One night recently, however, he went too far. I was in the shower, washing my hair, when I heard Ernie making a terrible screeching noise. Suddenly, out of the corner of my eye I saw a blur of dark fur and claws; it was above me, trying to balance on the shower curtain rod. I was worried about scratches as I was naked with a cat about to fall into the shower. I called for my husband to help, and reached up to help Ernie balance himself. Because I was wet he shrank away from me, making the entire situation worse. It really only lasted a matter of seconds, but time seemed to have slowed down. Luckily, my husband recognised the frenzied call in my voice, and came in to save the day. Now Ernie stands outside the bathroom door making little worried noises when any of us are in the shower.

Harry the Daredevil
Jeanette, 32

I got my cat Harry about four years ago. A friend of a friend was moving abroad and couldn't take her cat with her so wanted him to have a good home. At the time, Harry was only about one year old so I thought that he might settle into a new home quite well.

When I first got him, he spent a week wandering around my

house meowing; probably missing his previous owner. I got him all the treats I could and after being thoroughly spoiled for a few weeks he finally accepted that living with me was going to be fine.

Harry is a daredevil. He jumps on everything, jumps off of everything, and bites through anything. He likes to rip up the newspapers if you leave them on the floor. It sometimes seems that he's got a bit of a death wish; he's jumped out of the first floor window but was unhurt when he landed in the garden. I don't like to think about how many lives he's got left.

I have a 'birthday party' for him every year to celebrate the day he came to live with me. I tell him how much I enjoy living with him. In return he tells me to feed him. I don't think that will ever change.

Moggs and the Dogs
Keith, 33

We got Moggs as a kitten for my daughter when she was five years old. We already had two large sheepdogs but I promised Lily that she could have a pet of her own. I was initially worried about how the dogs would react to our tiny new furry housemate but they were absolutely fine with her. They even let Moggs steal their dog food now and again.

I always take the dogs for a walk at around 6.30pm. They look forward to it and start whimpering and running back and forth from the kitchen door by about 6.20. After she had lived with us for a few months, Moggs began to join in with the excitement. She would meow and then follow the dogs to and from the door. It wasn't long before I opened the kitchen door and Moggs ran out with the dogs.

She was going out and exploring the area by this time, so I thought it would be interesting to see how far she came on the walk with us.

Moggs followed us down the garden path and out into the lane. She just galloped along like the dogs. Every so often they would get ahead of her and then they'd run back to her as if they were involving the cat in their game.

Our walk takes us through a farmyard, where Moggs trotted along the side of the building and ran across the yard chasing the dogs. Then she ran up the hill toward the cypress trees and into the woods. The dogs love snuffling through the leaves in the woods and Moggs was quite happy to watch them. She sat on a soft bed of leaves and calmly watched the dogs snuffling and grunting along the woodland floor.

I've been escorting Moggs and the dogs each day after work and, recently, have realised I am bonding with our cat. I had thought of Moggs as my daughter's cat and didn't expect that I would have that much to do with her, but since she began coming on our walks, I am learning so much about this sweet little animal. She loves climbing high into trees, eating insects, and sniffing where the squirrels have been in the grass. It really is wonderful to watch her. Watching Moggs, I've discovered that she's an agile hunter who imagines that falling leaves are animals to chase and catch. She enjoys rubbing against the rough barks of the oak trees. I've also noticed she's becoming more confident at climbing and hiding. Our daughter adores our cat, too. She's now eight years old and, during school holidays, often accompanies us on our walk, playing fetch with Moggs and the dogs.

One day however, all did not go to plan. We were walking through the woods as usual but when Moggs ran off to explore she didn't come back. I looked everywhere, but I couldn't find her. She seemed to have vanished. I searched for Moggs in all of her favourite places up the tall trees and in the bramble bushes. I would have thought that the dogs would have found her but they were just running in circles.

I searched and searched. It was getting darker and colder. I thought about the stray dogs and foxes in the area. I was worried that they might attack her. I walked back up the hill to the cypress trees again and peered into the woods, shouting "Moggs, Moggs"!

That's when I heard something very faint on the breeze. It was a very high pitched meow and seemed to be coming from far away. I walked further into the woods but the sound became fainter. I walked back to the edge of the woods and the sound got stronger. I looked around trying to work out where the noise was coming from. It was quite windy so it was hard to pinpoint the direction but it seemed to be coming from the other side of the cypress trees.

I walked around the cypress trees and crouched down on the ground. The noise got louder, it seemed to be coming from the ground but all I could see was grass. On this side, the hill was more ridged and from here I could hear Moggs clearly. I walked down the hill slowly and found a bank of rabbit holes. This was where the sound was coming from. I went to each hole in turn and called for Moggs. She meowed back at me clearly from the third one. She must have run in there and got stuck as the soil fell down behind her. I started to make the hole wider using my hands as shovels; the soil was very sandy so it wasn't too difficult. Eventually I created a large enough hole to see Moggs little face peering out at me. I reached in and gently pulled her out, worried that she might be injured.

However, once I got her out she seemed fine. The dogs were delighted to get her back and both licked her face in happiness. I think they couldn't get her scent because she had fallen too far down the rabbit hole. I was just so relieved that she was safe.

In the Dryer
Megan, 49

About six months ago, I was passing by the utility room and saw that the tumble dryer door was slightly open. It reminded me that I needed to dry the clothes I'd taken out of the washing machine so I picked up the basket where the wet clothes were and tipped the contents into my dryer and switched it on. Next I collected some more dirty clothes to put into the washing machine. While I was filling the washer with the dirty towels I heard a faint meow. I looked around the room for a few seconds before I realised that the sound was coming from inside the dryer. My heart was in my mouth as I switched off the dryer and opened the door. I could see my cat Horace's tail sticking up out of a mountain of clothes. I was so worried that I'd hurt him. He must have jumped into the machine without me noticing.

Thankfully he was unharmed and seemed more angry than scared but it gave me such a fright. I cuddled him and petted his head telling him how sorry I was. I laid him on the sofa and examined him more closely but he didn't seem to be injured at all. I only had the dryer on for a minute maybe two at the most and I think all the clothes cushioned the tumbles for him. I was so relieved. I thought about calling the vet but Horace immediately went back to his boisterous and naughty behaviour, running about the house, stuffing his face with cat food and sunbathing on the window sill. It was like nothing had happened. I'm just so glad I heard him and got him out in time. I don't want to think about what would have happened if I hadn't decided do some more washing and, instead, just walked out of the utility room.

Jim
Roger, 44

My cat Jim once saved me from a potential fire. I was renting a house with electrical issues, the fuses were always blowing. One night I was tired & was dozing off on the couch. As I fell asleep, Jim came over and started meowing at me. I ignored him because I was sleepy but he was persistent; he tried again and again. He ran over to the door and ran back to me, meowing. I tried to sleep but he wouldn't let me. Jim's meows got louder and louder until he jumped onto my chest and rubbed his face over mine. I finally woke up and made for the door to see what Jim had got so agitated about. This time I followed where he was looking and I could see smoke.

I had an extension cord behind a dresser and it was smoking. As I moved the sideboard a spark shot out at me, which I quickly stamped out. There was smoke all over the room. I yanked out the plug and then picked up Jim and went next door to call the fire brigade. If I had fallen asleep there may have been a serious fire, we both may have died. I lost Jim many years ago but I still think of that night.

Magical and Amazing Cats

Cats have always been associated with superstitions, such as the one about black cats crossing your path. But some of these stories go beyond superstition, to strange observations, spiritual connections and omens. Here we find cats who sit in circles, who arrive in mysterious circumstances, or whose behaviour seems hard to explain in normal terms.

Comfort Cookie
Vera, 54

I am sure that my cat Cookie has saved me several times. I got her and her sister Pie, when they were kittens. I am a diabetic and one night, I was having difficulty breathing and also had chest pains. She seemed to sense it right away and came into my room, jumped on my bed and laid across my chest where she remained for about thirty minutes until the pain stopped and I was able to breathe again. Another time, I had quite severe abdominal pains and she came and got on my bed and lay across my stomach, purring as hard as she could for about twenty minutes. The pain stopped but for the rest of the week she would come and lie in my bed with me till she knew I was fine. She is very vocal and I am beginning to read her signs and her meows when it comes to my health. I had a heart attack in 2002 after having a very stressful year but I thank God every day for her. Pie doesn't take as good care of me as her sister. But I love them both so much and I am so glad that they are in my life.

Ghostly Cat
Allie, 22

I'm sure I once saw the ghost of my cat. My cat Tottins who was a large tabby cat, died about a year ago and I miss him badly. He was always sitting with me and rubbing his ears against my arms. He was hit by a car and left beside the road. My dad buried him in our back garden.

Two days after he died I heard a meowing at the kitchen door and thinking it was a stray I went to shoo it away. I looked through the stained glass in the back door and I could see a cat the exact size, colour and build of Tottins. I remember my heart beating as I struggled to get the back door open. When I opened the door, there was no one there but I saw a flash of tabby fur disappear around the side of the garage. I followed but again there was nothing to see. I'm still convinced that it was Tottins coming to say goodbye properly.

Morsel
Cathy, 28

I think that to truly understand cats you have to have lived with one. Not only do they reflect any happiness you give them, they also seem to know when something is wrong.

A few years ago on a rainy Monday morning, an hour after my boyfriend had gone to work, I was just crawling out of bed. Although I had been suffering from a very bad cough, I felt fine when I walked out of my bedroom and went to the kitchen and got myself a drink of juice. I have a huge ginger cat called Morsel who weighs getting on for 15 lbs and every morning he comes up to me rubbing around my legs and shouting for food. My parents had got a young female cat when I left home, and she had kittens a little while later. So I decided that I wanted to take in one of the little kittens.

I had had Morsel for almost four years by this point, and my younger cat Biscuit was only about a year old. Biscuit was always lying asleep on the sofa but Morsel never left my side. He followed me into the bathroom but on this day, when I got in there, I started feeling dizzy. I tried to go back into the living room to get the phone but I didn't make it out of the doorway before I fainted on the bathroom floor.

I don't remember much about that day or for the five days after, since I was put in the hospital in intensive care and I was drifting in and out of consciousness. But I have been told that Morsel saved my life. He was meowing and licking my face and pawing at me so that somehow I managed to call my mum who immediately called for an ambulance. I had a severe chest infection that had caused a very bad case of pneumonia. My mum (who has a key), told me that Morsel stayed by my side waiting for the ambulance and licking my face.

Even when I got home from the hospital two weeks later, Morsel followed me about showing a lot of concern for my well being. It is wonderful to know that your cat loves you and that he will return in kind all the care you give to him.

Saved By a Cat
Barry, 65

My life was saved by a cat when I was two years old. I was playing in the back garden when an old tree lost one of its branches. Just before it fell, our cat Toby leapt on me and bit my arm, making me start to cry and run off to get the attention of my mum. If he hadn't done that the branch would have fallen directly on top of me.

Ever since that day, I have always had a very close connection with animals, especially cats. I know from numerous experiences animals help us heal in every way, emotional, physical and mental. I have always had a strong passion for animal rescue work also and over the years I have adopted eight cats.

I am now sixty five years old and I have had two heart attacks over the past ten years. I am convinced that each time my cats have helped to lower my blood pressure and make me physically stronger.

Cat Spirits
Mavis, 23

I'm a very spiritual person and my spirits are three cats. It's strange because I don't especially like cats and I have two dogs, so why my spirits are cats I don't know.

The first cat I call my comforter. Whenever I'm in bed, I can feel him walking around on top of my bedcovers. Sometimes I can make out his shape quite clearly. He is black and white and when I'm asleep he climbs onto my stomach and sits there. I have become quite fond of this cat and find him quite amusing when he does his little tricks to wake me up, like when he bites my nose and my toes.

Then one day when I was lying on my bed half asleep I felt another cat on the other side of me. This cat just lies alongside of me and I get the sense that his is the spirit that protects me. Shortly after that experience another cat spirit came to me and likes to play with my hair.

A Circle of Cats
Debbie, 28

I was on my way from work one dark winter's night when I saw a strange sight. In the doorway of an abandoned house I saw a circle of cats. They were all sitting facing inwards towards the circle and didn't appear to be making much noise. It was a very odd thing to witness. All the cats were sitting upright in exactly the same position and all had their ears pointed forward as if their business was with each other.

I have told this story to friends many times. I'm always asked how many cats there were but I have to say, I didn't count. Some people think that if there were seven it was a witches coven or if there were six it was a meeting of evil but I don't believe any of that. Having said that though, I still have no idea what they were up to.

An Angel Cat
Harvey, 48

I was standing with two friends by the churchyard one day during the first week of June having a chat when suddenly a cat came strolling across the street. It was one of those short-haired bluey-grey cats that look like velvet. It walked right up in front of me, looked up at me and meowed.

My friends were laughing at me because they know that I don't like cats. I walked a few steps away and continued my conversation. The cat walked over to me again and just as before, looked up at my face and meowed. My friends were now laughing hysterically and we went though the same scenario a few times. Each time the cat simply followed, stared at me and meowed.

Eventually one of my friends picked up the cat and handed it to me. I couldn't think why the cat was interested in me but I decided to take it home to see if it really wanted to be with me as much as it seemed to. There was a collar around its neck that said Freddo so I called it that. At home I gave Freddo some food, water and soon we were becoming friends. In fact, I thought he acted more like a dog; he responded to his name, loved being petted and would come running when I called him. Freddo and I got very attached to each other.

A couple of months later, my family and I went on holiday for a week. When we returned, I could not find Freddo anywhere. I searched and searched and couldn't find him. I waited a day or so and then went knocking on my neighbours doors. I had grown so fond of him and missed him so much.

Later that afternoon, a neighbour knocked on my door and said, "I have to tell you the truth, your cat was taken in by a neighbour down the street. It got out of your house and was meowing to be let back in all night." I asked the man where the cat was now. He said that the cat had misbehaved at the neighbours' house and they had given the cat to him to look after.

I was so relieved to know that Freddo was safe; I asked the man if I could have my cat back. However, the man told me that his son has severe asthma and reacted terribly to the cat. So the man had given it to a friend who lived about six miles away. Initially I was quite annoyed, because he was obviously someone's pet. The man told me that they had been desperate to find the cat somewhere to stay and told me that his friend had a son with leukaemia and he had fallen in love with Freddo and wanted him to stay. I relented and said that if he really loved the cat his friend's son could keep it. I let it be known that I was always ready to keep the cat again if they grew fed up with him

A couple of months later, the neighbour came to my door again and told me what had happened. The little boy had died over the weekend. He said that from the moment the boy and the cat were together they were inseparable. The night the little boy died he had been slipping in and out of consciousness and all he wanted was to cuddle the cat. Freddo stayed with the boy and he had died with Freddo in his arms. After the doctor had been called and the boy was confirmed dead the cat disappeared and hadn't been seen since. It had apparently run off into the woods.

The following week Freddo turned up on my doorstep, a little dirty and scruffy but otherwise fine. He seemed to have decided that his job with the little boy was over and he could come home. I think that Freddo was a gift from God for the little boy and we will never know why it had to take the strange route that it took in order to get to him but I will never forget it. I like to think that Freddo was a ministering angel. The kind a little boy would understand and want to be close to.

Sixth Sense
Richard, 17

Our cat Polo must have a sixth sense, because he always knows when someone is coming home. I've seen him do it loads of times, his ears prick up and he gets up looking all perky and then trots out the cat door to wait on the path. He does this when either of my parents or my sister are on their way home, and if I come home he is always out there waiting.

You'd think he just has good hearing, but I've seen him do it whether people are on foot or in the car, and for me it is often when I am on my bike. I've tried creeping up to the house as quietly as possible and still he is always there. And it isn't right at the last minute, either. He knows about five or ten minutes before someone gets there. The only time I have seen him miss someone getting home is when he is fast asleep and twitching his legs in a dream.

I know it sounds silly but I really can't think of any other way of understanding it than to think that he has some kind of psychic connection to us all and just knows when we are on our way.

A Psychic Cat
Carol, 32

A nutritionist I used to be friendly with had a cat that she insisted was psychic. She said that the cat seemed to know when her clients needed some help. She would sit outside the therapy room and meow loudly until allowed in. Then she would jump straight on to the person and curl up quietly. After a while she would leave and go away quietly. She said that without exception, her clients were happy with this. It probably also brought her more business.

Jeremy's Double
Katya, 27

When I was ten, my mother brought home a tabby cat that a co-worker of hers gave her. Before bringing him home, she showed me a picture and I instantly fell in love. He was so sweet with brown stripes over his face and large green eyes. His name was Jeremy. After bringing him home, he immediately became attached to me and followed me everywhere. He was always doing funny and unusual things that made us laugh. We had never had a cat before, and he made us laugh so much with his antics.

I lived with my parents until I went off to university. I really wanted to take him with us, but couldn't. My parents were too attached to him, and I couldn't have kept him in my college rooms anyway. I got to see him on almost a weekly basis though, because I usually went home or visited at weekends.

Sadly, Jeremy died last year at the ripe old age of sixteen. He got a tumour in his stomach and there was nothing the vet could do for him. I went with my father to take him to the vet to have him put to sleep. It was one of the hardest things I've had to do. I have a four year old daughter who kept looking for him because she couldn't understand why he wasn't coming back.

We still reminisce and miss him very much. A few months ago, my sister-in-law's cat had a litter of kittens; one of them looked very similar to Jeremy. When the kittens were about 3 months old, I took that kitten home. I had this strange, compelling desire to take him. My children and I were so happy after bringing him home, and it didn't take long to notice the kitten who we named Jimmy began doing things just the way my old Jeremy did. The strange, funny things he used to do, that no other cat we've seen do, this kitten does.

Cat Security
Dean, 35

One very cold winter night, my wife and I were asleep upstairs unaware that a burglar was trying to get into our home through the side window of the house in an otherwise unobserved lane. He must have watched the house for long enough to be sure that we did not have a dog.

He managed to remove the screen that covered our downstairs hall window and lever open the window from the closure. What he didn't know about was our very large and stroppy tortoiseshell cat, Beattie, who isn't very keen on strangers; especially ones who arrive through windows in the middle of the night.

At some point after he climbed through the window, Beattie went into action. She screeched out a yowl and went for him. She can be quite scary when she is distressed, all her fur stands on end and her tail becomes as fat as a foxes. At this point, the burglar screamed, and my wife and I woke up. He probably had no idea what kind of animal was attacking him in the dark.

I ran downstairs with my heart beating. All I could see was someone scrambling their way back out through the window while Beattie kept on making a hell of a racket. I think that the speed with which she acted must have taken the burglar totally by surprise.

Whilst all this was going on my wife was phoning the police from upstairs and pretty soon we could see blue flashing lights and hear sirens outside. As they took our statements the police couldn't help smiling. They said that they knew of plenty of burglaries that had been disrupted by dogs but they had never encountered a cat in that role!

It was lucky she did, as otherwise he would have found his way into the study where we keep our laptops, desk computer and my wife's photographic equipment. Since then we have installed burglar alarms and beefed up the security. It's a horrible feeling having someone try to break in, but it's good to know we have such a good watch cat waiting for anyone who tries again. I don't think that particular burglar will be coming back our way in a hurry, at least.

The Spirit of Paws
Helen, 40

Mt next door neighbour Jessie had a black and white cat called Paws, which she was always fussing over. The two of them were very close and you could see how much she loved him. He was a friendly cat and was all over me whenever I went round for a visit.

I went round one day to find Jessie in tears. She told me that the vet had told her that Paws had a malignant tumour. She had taken him to the vet because he had stopped eating and looked so slumped and unhappy. I looked at Paws sitting in his basket by the radiator. He was clearly not his usual boisterous self. I told her how sorry I was and that she could always come round to see me if she didn't want to be on her own.

About two weeks later I got back from a few days away and saw Paws in Jessie's window looking remarkably well. He had gained some weight and was washing himself vigorously. Thinking that he must have been miraculously cured I knocked on Jessie's door. She looked shocked when I told her what I had seen. She told me that Paws had passed away two days before. She told me that she had initially refused to have him put to sleep at the vets because she wanted him to die at home with her by his side. However, Paws seemed to be in more and more pain every day so eventually she had called out the vet who had put him to sleep at home.

I told her that it was almost certainly the spirit of Paws who had come back for a visit because he had loved living with her.

Petal the Protector
Billy, 39

My cat Petal was the bravest little cat in the world. I was violently abused as a child and he used to try and protect me from the blows by biting and scratching the person who was attacking me. Afterwards, he would cuddle up with me and I felt like I was not so alone. I think he really did his best to look out for me and we were very close.

Sunny Meadows
Kerry, 59

I have loved all the cats I ever had and when I die I hope I can meet them again. I read a story when I was little that described a place where an animal goes when they die if they had a human that they were particularly close to. There were meadows and hills and trees, so that the animals could run and play, and plenty of their favourite foods. All the animals who had died of illness were back to being young and healthy again and the weather was always warm.

Although they were happy, all the animals had one thing in common; they all missed the human who had taken care of them and they were waiting for them. When the human who had looked after them died, they were together again for ever. I hope the story is true and I can be with my beautiful cats again.

Rescue Cats

It is good to see how many people rescue stray cats, either by taking them from a rescue centre or by helping out a cat that has been lost or abandoned. Grown-up cats face particular problems when they need rescuing as people often prefer to adopt a kitten, but there can be a real joy in helping a cat of any age.

Hans
Louise, 25

I would like to share my story about my beautiful long-haired male cat named Hans. When I was a child we always had cats but I developed a mild allergy to them in my teens and after that I didn't have any cats for years, but when I moved to a new town I felt quite lonely at first and so I decided to risk getting a cat.

I got Hans from a rescue centre. There were so many cats and kittens there that needed a new home but the one I felt most connected to when I saw him was Hans. Until I saw him I was starting to feel a little sad, I had walked down a long hallway and when I turned the corner I saw an enormous cat in a cage. He had very long ginger fur and was so big he hardly fitted in the cage.

I looked at him and his big yellow eyes stared back at me. I said hello to him and he meowed an answer back and that was it. Hans was mine.

The staff at the shelter told me that he'd only come in that day after being found as a stray. They said that I had to wait seven days in case he was just lost and had a family somewhere looking for him. If no one had claimed him after seven days he could be mine.

At home I felt so impatient waiting for him. I actually called the shelter every day to see if he had been picked up and after seven days was overjoyed that no one had come to claim him. On the way back to the shelter I stopped to buy cat food, kitty litter, and a comfy cat cushion. When they handed Hans to me he began to purr and I was instantly in love.

Hans is a graceful, affectionate and proud cat. He enjoys his own company but will always give you love and affection any time you pick him up or cuddle him. He is also good with visitors and always greets them with a meow and rubs around them. As soon as I brought him home I felt less alone and the house seemed much brighter. Also, the strange thing is that I'm not allergic to him. He is perfect.

The Three-Pawed Cat
Clara, 19

Just before Christmas last year, a cat turned up on our doorstep meowing insistently. It was holding up its left paw as if it was begging. I shouted for my mum to come and look at it. She came and touched the cat's paw and it cried even louder. My mum said that it was probably swollen because it was injured and we'd have to take it to the vet.

We put the cat in a box and drove over to the vets. We told them that he wasn't our cat and by the state of him he was almost certainly a stray. The vet examined him and told us that his injured paw was badly infected and the only treatment was amputation. Since he wasn't our cat, the vet suggested that really he should be put to sleep because no one would adopt a disabled cat.

I begged and begged my mum to adopt him and she agreed there was something about him that was very endearing. He was white with grey tabby patches all over him and seemed to have a very sweet and gentle nature. We left him at the vet with instructions to collect him in forty-eight hours.

Two days later we brought home our three-pawed pet. At first he found it difficult to balance but once he worked out his three-legged hop he was absolutely fine. We called him Jim and other than missing a front paw, he's very healthy and happy.

He loves to cuddle, and spar with you. I'm so happy that we saved him.

Difficult Jay
Carol, 63

My cat Jay came from a cat rescue shelter. He seems mostly normal but he also has some strange behaviours. He'll talk to me while staring up at me from the floor as though he wants attention, but when I reach down to pet him he runs away. He does this unless he's high up on a counter, on the back of my sofa, or on my desk. When I give up trying to appease him he'll then jump up onto my desk unsatisfied with anything but my full attention including petting and scratching, disrupting my every attempt to reach my keyboard.

He sleeps at the foot of my bed at night and the only time he wants attention is when he's not sitting or lying on the floor. I've had lots of cats but never one who behaved like this.

Ruby, the Constant Companion
Rose, 44

I miss my cat Ruby. She was with us for twenty-two years and the whole time she was always with me. She watched me raise two children and was by my side during the break-up of my marriage.

I had to have her put to sleep two years ago and as the vet did his job she died in my arms. I was so sad. It was a very hard thing to do. I cried all the way home and I held a little burial service for her in the garden. She has a place of honour underneath the magnolia tree that she used to sit under in the spring, making yakking noises at the birds as they flitted in the branches.

I still mourn Ruby. She's left a big hole on my heart but I'm grateful to have known her and glad that she was in my life for so long. When she died I thought I would never love another cat.

My second husband said that when I felt up to it, we could adopt a cat or get another kitten. For a year I wasn't ready for that because all I could think about was my beloved Ruby. Then last May, a litter of kittens was born in my neighbour's garage and because they knew I was a cat lover, they came to me for help. The litter of four feral kittens seemed to have no mother. We tried to bottle feed them but only two survived and they were fed in my neighbour's garden. Four weeks later my neighbour went on holiday and asked me to care for the kittens while she was away. I had allowed the remaining two to feed on my patio out of Ruby's dishes sometimes so it wasn't much of an imposition.

One morning it was raining heavily so I left the back door open to try and persuade the kittens to come inside. They came trotting in and I put the food bowls on the kitchen floor. It was important to me that they were eating and out of the cold rain. As I watched their tiny heads bob up and down as they ate the food something stirred in me and I felt ready to share my home with cats once again. When my neighbour came home, I asked her if I could adopt the kittens and to my delight she said yes.

A few weeks later as spring returned I stood in the kitchen and watched Pogo and Bess playing under the magnolia tree. Two blackbirds were chasing each other around the branches and the kittens were crouched low underneath it squeaking at them.

Mow the Bouncy Cat
Ella, 13

I have a female cat called Mow that I got from an animal shelter. I think she's about three years old.

I'm only thirteen but she has made me so much happier. She jumps up and down and literally bounces off the wall for no reason even though she's absolutely huge and very tubby. She has a meow so high-pitched that it could probably break glass if she was loud enough.

Mow sleeps right next to me and waits for me in the morning. She jumps up and down like a little dog when I make her breakfast. She gives me reassurance and company. She only loves me and my family and she hates everyone else, she growls and hisses when we have visitors. Every time we put a collar on her, she manages to lose it so we've given up buying them for her.

She drinks water from the fishbowl and deliberately goes to the toilet right after her litter tray has been cleaned. She is entertained by anything small or anything that moves.

Mow sleeps on all my important homework papers and refuses to let me get at them to do my work. She can literally jump three feet in the air and can get out onto our roof. She also loves biting my necklace if she comes to sit on me. I love her.

Missing Bluebell
Maisy, 62

My cat Bluebell, died about two months ago. I knew she was ill but it was worse than I had imagined. At first she had difficulty breathing, I thought that maybe she just had a cold. I wish I had taken her to the vet immediately but other than the weird breathing, she seemed fine. I didn't make an appointment with the vet for three weeks and in that time her condition worsened. She lost a lot of weight and then suddenly collapsed, breathing though her mouth and drooling. I took her to the vet who said that Bluebell had chronic kidney disease and there was nothing he could do.

The vet advised me to have Bluebell put to sleep and I reluctantly agreed. But now I wonder if I could have waited a little longer to see if she'd get better. I can't help but think it was too early for her to leave me. Bluebell used to curl up with me on bed and purr, and I miss her so much. It's horrible not to have her waiting for me when I get home. I don't know her real age as I got her from the people who originally adopted her as a stray after they weren't able to care for her because she didn't get along with their other cats so I don't know if it was complications from age.

It's just sad and I wish she was still around, but she isn't. I still have her water dish and food dish and litter box, that's all I have of her now. I really miss having Bluebell around.

Lucy
Veronica, 56

When my last two cats died I didn't get another cat for about four years. They were seventeen and eighteen years old and got sick within a matter of months of each other and had to be put to sleep. It broke my heart and I felt like I'd never be able to replace them.

However, four years later I woke up one morning and decided that it was time that I got a new cat. I went to a local shelter and checked online for cats at other nearby shelters. So many cats need homes; it was so hard to choose one. Then I saw a picture online and went to see Lucy at a shelter about six miles from my town. She had been found wandering the streets, pregnant, and someone had taken her to the animal shelter. Homes had been found for the kittens, but not for her.

The minute I saw Lucy, with her bedraggled black fur and her beautiful yellow eyes, I knew she would be coming home with me. She was one year old then, and I've had her for five wonderful years now. She is the best cat and a great pet. From a scrawny, thin cat, she has grown into a beautiful, shiny and fluffy lady. She always snuggles up to me and we watch TV together. She sleeps on my bed and makes little chirpy noises in the morning when she decides she's hungry. I have a cat door so she's not a house-bound cat but she never goes far from home. I think that she's happy that I gave her a home. I know I'm happy to have her.

Broken Blinds
Julie, 26

I have a three year old cat named Zack. He is a ginger-striped cat with white paws and belly, and he has a ginger-striped tail.

Zach is a rescue cat who was found on the street after a really bad storm, and taken to an animal rescue centre. When he was two and I lived in a second floor flat, he would always sit looking out of the window at the world passing by outside. It was his favourite form of amusement.

Late one night I was watching TV when I heard a screech and a noise that sounded like paper crushing up. I went to my bedroom and found that my window was open and the blinds had been destroyed.

I ran outside to find Zach sitting on the ground still tangled up in the blinds, hissing and screeching at me. He must have miscalculated his jump onto the window sill and got tangled up in them. After untangling him and receiving a few scratches in return, I took him back inside.

He still gets on to the window sill, but he is much more careful about how he jumps up now. I haven't bothered replacing the blinds; I didn't like them much anyway.

Sox
Helena, 32

I found my cat Sox when he was just a young cat, not much more than a kitten. I used to see him wandering round the neighbourhood when I was taking my daughter to school. He was black with four white paws. You could tell that he was a stray because he was always quite thin and very bedraggled looking.

One day, one of the other mothers picked him up from under a hedge and told me that she was going to take him to a rescue centre. I looked at his little face and tiny white paws and just had to say that I'd keep him. I put him into my shopping bag where he seemed to be happy enough and carried on to the school. On my way home, I talked to him and he made occasional little meows back at me. That afternoon I put him in a box and took him to the vet and got him sorted out for fleas and all those sorts of things.

He really settled well into my family and my daughter absolutely adores him. He's now much bigger and looks so much healthier. He scampers around and has a naughty shoe chewing habit that I'm trying to discourage him from pursuing. I don't know how he became a stray but from the looks of him now it doesn't seem to have done too much damage.

Poppy and Weasel
Suzanna, 27

A few years ago some children came to my friend's house with a box full of four kittens and a very thin stray mother cat. They said they had found them close to the post office. She already had a cat so they had thought that she might know what to do with them. However, she also had two children under three years old and could not take care of the kittens as well so she asked if I would be able to deal with them. I telephoned quite a few animal shelters but no one had any room for them so I took them in myself.

I had the mother spayed and called her Poppy and looked after her while she fed them when they were very tiny. At about nine weeks old they were beginning to eat solid food and the mother cat weaned them off her. I found homes for three of the kittens and so was left with one and Poppy, who had settled in with me really well. The kitten is black with white socks and he's called Weasel because he's always hiding behind the furniture and peeping out slyly. It was just this strange course of events that led me to owning cats; I would never have thought to get a cat before all that.

Snowdrop and Boyo
Helena, 28

A few years ago, my husband and I decided to get a couple of cats and went to a local cat rescue centre to pick two out. We wanted rescue cats, specifically older ones that perhaps no one else wanted. I had told my husband that we were not getting long haired cats because I didn't want to have cat hair all over our house.

After looking at all the cats and not finding any who we wanted to take home with us, the manager of the shelter told us that they had two more cats in a room off the reception area who hadn't been processed yet and we could have a look at those two if we wanted.

In the room were two Persian cats. The male was a greyish colour and was clearly very scared; he was just shaking in a corner of his cage. The female, who was all white, was curled up in a corner. Apparently they had been left by the roadside in a cardboard box in the middle of the cold January weather. The female growled and hissed at everyone. The manager said she thought they would be difficult to find homes for because of their behaviour, and that they might be a bit of a challenge, but she wondered if we'd be interested in giving them a home.

I sat down in the room with them and in less than a minute, the male came over to me and settled into my lap purring. He looked as if he didn't want to move. I was completely covered in fur. The little female was huddled in the corner and when we tried to talk to her, she just growled at us. But, suddenly, there was no question; we were going to take these two Persian cats home. So much for my initial objection to long haired cats; we were now going to have two of them.

The shelter manager was so happy that we were taking both of them. I think she was relieved at the speed in which she'd managed to find them a home.

It has now been two years since they came to live with us and I can't imagine life without them. Boyo, the male cat, is the most affectionate cat I have ever met. He follows me around the house, he comes to me when he's called, he loves to play with me, he sleeps with me and he curls up with me when I read or watch TV. The little girl, Snowdrop was quite fierce for the first few weeks, but then she seemed to decide that we were acceptable owners and now she has also become a really sweet, loving cat. She greets me in the morning by rubbing her nose and mouth on my chin before settling down on my chest kneading away.

These two cats are the most adorable animals I have ever seen. They are both really fluffy. Boyo is huge and Snowdrop is still quite small but has a lot of fluffy white fur. I get great satisfaction when I see how healthy and happy they are now compared to when we first met them. Their eyes are shiny and bright and their fur is luxurious and silky. I think they're just as happy living with us as we are to have them.

My Cat
Gail, 29

We went to the shelter to see all the kittens, hoping to bring one home that day. There were so many it was really hard to choose. We already have two kids, so it was important that we got quite an outgoing cat because our house can be really noisy at times.

We found Sammy alone in his cage, he was black with a white bib on his chest and as we walked past he ran to the front of the cage and began meowing to us. We asked the assistant if she could let him out of his cage to meet us and she brought him to a table in a quiet room. He crawled up my arm and tucked himself under my chin and that was it, he had to come home with us.

He wasn't quite eight weeks old, so we had to wait another one and half weeks to get him. Eventually we brought him home and he fits in perfectly with our family. The children love him dearly, and my husband who isn't entirely a cat person, is very fond of him too. He is the family cat, but of course secretly he's become "my cat".

Missy
Caroline, 26

I never intended to get a cat, it happened by accident. The people who used to live across the street from me moved out and left the poor little thing behind. She was just a kitten, not much more than three months old. She is all black and the cutest little animal in the world. I named her Missy. I don't know why but it kind of fits her; she's a stroppy little madam. Still, I can't believe that someone would just leave a poor little kitten to survive on its own.

When we first got Missy she was very weak, it took her about a month to feel comfortable with us and her new situation. She did eventually become very playful. Then, disaster struck. Missy ate something that had been poisoned and was very ill.

We took her to the vet who said he didn't think there was much that he could do and told us to take her home and keep her comfortable and warm and give her water but no food. I had a sleepless night worrying and praying that she would be OK. My prayers were answered and next morning she seemed a little brighter. I left her quietly sleeping on her blanket and went to work. When I got home that evening she was almost back to her normal cheeky self and immediately began admonishing me for not giving her anything to eat. I put a bowl of food down and she ate it almost without taking a breath. Since that day she has stopped bringing home rodents (but she still goes after birds) so we wonder if it might have been a rat or mice that had been poisoned that she ate. If so it is pretty smart of her to avoid them now.

Kind to Old Ladies
Troy, 44

In about 1990 I adopted a cat from a rescue centre. He was black with a white patch on top of his head and his name was Sooty. He was about six months old when I got him and although he seemed to settle in well he was always making that kind of plaintive meow noise that cats make when they are calling for each other. After a couple of months I decided to get him a companion. The rescue centre advised me to get him a sister rather than a brother as two male cats may become aggressive with each other, so eventually I took home a young black cat called Lily. The two of them became great friends and chased each other round my flat all day, hiding behind doors and playing at pouncing on the other as he or she came through it. The three of us were very happy together for about four years until I got a job offer from a company in Paris. The job would mean moving to France for the foreseeable future and I knew that I could not take my cats.

My parents have a large house with a very big garden and I knew that they loved cats so I asked them if I could leave Lily and Sooty with them when I moved to Paris. They already had an old Burmese female called Queenie, but they agreed and I took my cats to live with them. Both cats took to the garden immediately and my parents told me that they spent most of the days outside chasing flies, bees and butterflies. Queenie however was initially furious about her space being invaded by two young alley cats. My cats were much larger than her but she would put up with no nonsense from them and gave each of them a slap and a hiss if they bothered her too much. Eventually she was rewarded with a lot of respect from them. The three of them lived happily together for the next ten years, sharing sleeping places when the weather was cold and playing in the garden during the summer

Queenie eventually died in her sleep, she was eighteen years old and my parents told me about how they found her in the kitchen with Sooty and Lily curled up around her. They were clearly upset by her death and became quiet and withdrawn for a few days, sitting in places where they had all sat together.

My parents eventually decided to help them out by getting a stroppy old tortoiseshell cat from a rescue centre. She was immediately angry at the sight of Sooty and Lily and order was subsequently restored once again.

Affectionate Stray
Jodie, 34

I saved my Thomas from a tragic end. The poor cat used to turn up at an old friend's farm and despite the many attempts she made to re-home him, he would always return back to her house. In the end she was talking about having him put to sleep. He was hopelessly scrawny and scruffy-looking. I'm a real animal lover and I couldn't bear the thought of that, so I bundled him up in a towel, fleas and all and took him home. I could not have asked for a better little friend. Even though he's been living wild for a long time, he has never once bitten, hissed or scratched. He is the most affectionate animal I have ever owned.

Injured By the Road
Mary, 58

One night, when my husband and I were driving home through heavy snow, we saw something large and white lying by the roadside. For a moment we didn't notice it as it was so well camouflaged, but there was a bit of redness and movement there too, which made us stop and investigate.

We pulled over and went to see what it was and discovered a large white cat. He was clearly in pain and there was blood on one of his hind legs. We couldn't just leave him there and our eldest son is a vet, so we picked the cat up gently and put him in the car. When we got home we called our son Joe, who is a vet, and he said he'd pop round to take a look at it. On closer inspection the cat was clearly feral or had been a stray for quite a long time. He was ragged looking, his white fur was stuck together in clumps and he was very thin.

Joe arrived about twenty minutes later and we put the cat on the kitchen table on a towel. Joe examined him and said that it looked like his leg was broken but other than that he was just malnourished. He gave the cat a little dose of anaesthetic and then re-set his leg before putting a cast on it. Joe said that the cat would wake up after about half an hour and gave us some antibiotics to give the cat, to ward off infection, then left. My husband and I discussed taking him to an animal shelter when he was better.

When he woke up, the cat began to meow. I was worried that it was the pain but then my husband suggested feeding him and we gave him a tin of sardines and a saucer of milk. He wolfed down both in a matter of seconds and then seemed to have calmed down. He curled up being very careful of his injured leg, and went back to sleep. He was still sleeping when we went to bed so we left him there.

The next morning, when I went into the kitchen, he set off meowing as he had the night before. This time I took some slices of ham from the fridge and gave them to him with a bowl of water. He ate as if he hadn't eaten in days.

When he'd finished I gave him a stroke and realised that I didn't want to take him to a rescue shelter and that I had become used to the idea of keeping him. I called him Snowball because he was white and had been found in a snow storm. He was completely relaxed with me and allowed me to give his fur a comb and scratch him behind his ears. I had never had a cat before but looking after this one was easy, as if it was meant to be.

That was nearly ten years ago now and Snowball is an old, wise cat. He has his favourite armchair. He likes to sit on the back of it and look out of the window, watching birds. I can't imagine our house without him now.

Ginny the Rescue Cat
Carla, 26

My cat Ginny is so sweet and lovely. We got her from a rescue centre and at first she really didn't like being picked up but I was very patient with her and after a few months she would allow it... just. Still, you wouldn't call her a lap cat. She does like to sit beside you on the sofa, just not to actually sit on you. When people come to visit she hides from them at first but she does come out to say hello eventually. She's quite chubby but not quite in the too-fat danger zone. I do sometimes share my food with her though I know I'm not supposed to.

I've tried to play with her to get her to have more exercise as she is an indoor cat but she's a very lazy lady. She will remain on the floor so you have to step over her rather than move to get out of your way. She loves lying on the sofa though and I like to sit with her and scratch the soft fur around her ears. She's a good cat and never scratches the furniture. I bought her a scratch post that hangs on the wall and she actually uses it. I've never known a cat to actually use them before. Because she's such a good girl I buy her catnip from time to time; it's good fun to watch her rolling around the floor.

Haunted Holly
Rob, 35

When I first moved to the country after years of city living, I wanted to get a pet. I decided on a cat because I had cats as a child and always really loved them. I went to the local rescue centre and in a cage I saw the most adorable little black cat. She stared at me with big yellow eyes and when the assistant took her out of the cage she allowed me to hold her, and purred and licked my nose. She was so affectionate and vocal that I just had to take her home with me. I decided to call her Holly as it was close to Christmas time.

Holly's now seven years old and is such a lovely cat to have around. She loves both people and other cats, which I found strange because female cats are known for not getting on with each other. She chases me around the house to play and when new neighbours moved in next door she spent a week going round there to get to know them. I think they like her too and she gets the odd treat from them.

It's funny because I live in quite an old Victorian house on a road with a school at the end of it and I hear the children talking as they go to school. Holly sometimes sits at the top of the steps leading up to my door and the children seem to believe that means the house is haunted. I always know when she's outside watching them because the children whisper, squeal and giggle. Holly isn't a scary black cat at all but I suppose children tend to invent things for fun.

Solitary Sid
George, 27

I got a stray kitten after a neighbour found that a stray cat had given birth to kittens in her garage. There were four of them and they were all scared at first, hissing and spitting at us. I took one of the kittens and other neighbours took the others. My new kitten was a little black male kitten and I called him Sid. Even though he was hissing and spitting when I first got him, I thought that if I cared for him well, he would eventually come to like me. I was wrong!

Sid is now about eight months old and will not be stroked or petted. He prefers to be on his own. In fact, he acts as if he is nothing to do with me. I am the one who feeds him, changes his litter, and combs him; but he is definitely not grateful. He enjoys going outside and sneaks out whenever he gets the chance. I don't like him going out so I pick him up and bring him back inside. I'm certain that that is one of the reasons he is difficult with me.

The situation seems to be getting worse. If he wants to go outside and I won't let him, he attacks me; I get chased, bitten and scratched. He now hisses at me just for walking too close to him. I had him neutered at three months old thinking that would help but it hasn't. I would love to be able to cuddle him but I think that is never going to happen. I still feed him and speak gently to him even as he is hissing in my face. Maybe eventually he will realise that I mean him no harm.

Tiddler
John, 34

We used to feed many of the stray cats where we used to live. They were mostly friendly and happy animals. There was a pretty long-haired female cat that had three kittens. She was a good mother to two of them but she wouldn't have anything to do with one of them. If he tried to feed from her she would bite him or push him away. I felt so sorry for that little kitten.

We brought him in when he was about eight weeks old. His head was about the size of a walnut and you could see all of his ribs. He was dying from starvation. He hadn't been able to eat the adult cat food we put outside because he wasn't strong enough, and when we put out softer kitten food, the other cats would get to it before he could.

We wrapped him in a soft towel and fed him warmed milk. He would drink it then settle down to sleep. He seemed to like the warmth of the towel.

After two days you could tell a major difference. He was able to walk and he could get into the litter box. He began to be more alert and awake. After the first week he could jump onto the table, meow and was really playful. Now he's a year old and weighs around ten pounds; he's about three feet long from head to tail, and keeps us awake at night by jumping on our bed.

He is a bit spoiled and very affectionate. He is the man of the house. His name is Tiddler because of how small he was when we got him and he's the cutest cat I have ever seen. He is good with the kids and he has a very gentle heart. I'm so glad that we took him in.

Heart to Heart
Carol, 24

No matter where you live, pet cats are fantastic. I rescued two beautiful grey tabby adult cats just over a year ago and these two cats, Adam and Eve, became my world. Unfortunately Adam, the largest, (and dominant one of the two), became very ill, and despite our repeated trips to the vet and prescriptions of every type of treatment imaginable, we had to have him put to sleep. Since then, the formerly quite docile female, Eve, has become my constant companion. She is at my side all the time. She has helped me weather the worst depressions, and soothes any pangs of loneliness with her warmth and love. She is a very chatty cat and I although I don't speak 'Cat' I think we understand each other. Every night Eve jumps onto the bed with me, and snuggles up against my chest, especially close when I am feeling a bit down, as if she knows that that is where my heart is.

Second Chance
Cora, 56

When I was a child I had a pet Siamese cat called Rory. He was like my little shadow and followed me wherever I went, even to my friend's house up the road. I was devastated when he died and didn't think I would ever have another cat because he was so special to me. However, a few years later I was to find myself being a cat owner once again.

I took my grandmother to our local animal rescue centre because she was thinking of getting a dog to keep her company after my granddad had died. To get to the dogs we had to first go down the corridors where the cats were kept and as I walked past a grey paw shot out from between the bars and grabbed my sleeves. I turned around to find a grey tabby cat staring at me with large green eyes. I said "hello", and the cat meowed back at me and I walked on. In the next corridor my grandma fell in love with a little Jack Russell called Willy so we turned back to go to the reception where she could go about adopting the little dog. As we walked back along the cat corridor the same thing happened. A grey paw grabbed my arm and this time the meow was more insistent, it was as if he didn't want to let me go. I carefully extricated myself but I couldn't stop thinking about him as my grandmother talked to the reception staff. Eventually I asked about him. They told me that he had only just been brought in after being found alone on some open grassland. I was also told that they had named him Rory.

It felt like fate had eventually intervened. I had to keep this cat. When they brought him out he was looking at me with such wise eyes and I promised him that I'd take him home and look after him. Back at my house Rory II settled in like he'd lived there all his life.

He sleeps on my bed at night and wakes me by patting at my eyelids in the mornings. He sits and watches me while I shower and is waiting behind the door when I come home. I don't know if Rory I and Rory II are at all connected but I do know that I was meant to have this cat.

All Kinds of Cats

There were too many funny or touching stories sent in to include all of these in a single section, so here is another selection of amusing feline tales and escapades.

Bossface and Lily
Jeff, 27

I have two cats that have both lived with me for all of their lives; they were both born on my grandfather's farm but from separate litters by different cats. They are very different.

Bossface is a large, stripy, ginger boy cat and he knows how to get what he wants. The other is a little lady called Lily who is much daintier than Bossface and tends to watch his antics from behind the sofa. She has tabby markings.

I work in a bar and I bring home beer mats for Bossface to play with. He loves to chew them and he also likes to play fetch with them. If I throw a beer mat he is ready and waiting. He chases it, and then brings it back to me so that I can throw it again. When he's had enough he simply lies down on the floor and chews them into tiny pieces. Everyday I have to pick up little chewed up bits of beer mat from all over the house.

The funny thing is that although Lily watches all of this from a distance, once the beer mats are in pieces she loves to take long runs at them and skid along in a snow storm of chewed cardboard. Lily also loves for you to pile up the beer mats into a pile as high as you can. She then jumps from the sofa or cupboards straight onto the pile so that she slips around everywhere as they scatter. If Bossface is around he grabs them and runs off with them or he just gets stuck in and starts chewing.

They really are a bundle of fun and I think that because they've known each other forever, they complement each other very well in their behaviour and temperament.

Biro the Jealous Cat
Pat, 22

My cat Biro, is a very jealous cat. He's jealous of the laptop, the desktop, the television, me and my fiancé as well if we have a cuddle. His attitude is "no, don't cuddle each other, cuddle me! Don't kiss each other, kiss me!"

If either of us gets home from work late, Biro doesn't hesitate to let us know that he has been lonely and immediately insists on getting our attention. Whenever I sit working on my computer, he jumps up and rubs against the screen, claiming it as his, then walks in front of the computer and meows at me non-stop.

He really does hate it when we're paying attention to anything except him, unless he's found something better to do such as chewing our house plants or ripping up our sofa.

Cat Brawl
Debs, 28

I have four cats, each of which seems to compete for the title of dumbest cat ever. Still, I absolutely adore all of them.

Sing-Sing is a large male Siamese. He's obnoxious, jealous, and possessive. I love him, though. Toby is a striped tabby Maine Coon cat. He has lost some weight but is still huge from the stupid amount of food that he demands. He loves to splash in the sink with his paws. Lindy is a beautiful fluffy, white, Persian cat. She seems to be fond of sneezing in my face when she is sniffing it, spraying me with god knows what. Sue-Sue is a rescue cat. Her markings are grey tabby, and her fur is as soft as a rabbit's. She's also dreadfully temperamental, and seems to hate everyone, especially the other cats and sometimes me.

One day, Lindy had a large piece of pink wrapping tape stuck to her tail. She didn't seem to care, but the other cats were curious about it. Toby wanted to smell it, but Lindy kept turning in circles, so he had a hard time reaching it. Finally, Toby caught up with her and took a sniff. Immediately, his eyes got squinty, and his top lip curled up as he took a bite at it. Sadly, he missed the wrapping tape and bit her tail instead. Lindy let out a loud yowl and took a swipe at him with her paws. Toby staggered side ways in to Sing-Sing who immediately jumped on Toby's huge fluffy tail. Toby swung round to get Sing-Sing and in the process trampled over Sue-Sue who was so furious that she leapt onto the top of all of them biting anything she could, probably herself as well at times.

It was a full-on cat brawl. In spite of myself, I was laughing because the noises were so strange, growls and shrieks and wails and hisses. Eventually, I broke the fight up by going into the kitchen and shaking the cat biscuit box. They all ran into the kitchen and performed being on their best behaviour to get a treat. I wish I'd had a film camera to hand that day because it really was a funny sight.

My Cat Eats Fruit
Paula, 31

My cat likes eating fruit. I think that that is the strangest behaviour of any cat that I have known. She's a rescued kitten and she came to us when she was barely month and a half old. So she was basically used to eating whatever she could get and even though we give her the best cat food we can afford, she still has very strange eating habits. She really likes to eat fruit. If I have a piece of fruit she is straight over to me swiping at it with her paw. She will eat pears, oranges and apples. Her favourite fruit is bananas and if she catches me peeling a banana she will wheedle and miaow until I give her some of it. If I put some pineapple on a plate she will lick up the juice after it's finished. Everybody I tell this story to reacts with disbelief but it's true, she is a very odd cat.

Womble
Jake, 28

Womble is the coolest cat I have ever met. He is a gigantic tabby cat who takes no prisoners. His previous owners, one of whom used to work with me, were moving house to go to live in a retirement community and couldn't keep him any more so he came to live with us. He was two years old at the time. When he got to our house, as soon as I opened the pet carrier, he immediately threw himself on our other cat Pen, and gave her a smack on the nose. Needless to say, Pen was not impressed.

After a few days of hiding under the bed in the guest bedroom, Womble came out and started to become part of our family. Pen made her peace with him in the end and now they will happily sleep together on the same cushion.

My wife got home late one night and caught Womble perched on the edge of the toilet seat taking a pee in the toilet. We didn't catch him doing it again for weeks. Then, I got out of the shower one morning and there he was again sitting on the toilet doing his necessaries. In case you want to know – he doesn't flush afterwards.

Kicking Coco
Ben, 24

My cat, Coco kicks herself in the face. She lies on the floor, on her back and tries to grab her tail but always misses and her back legs kick her in the face. No matter how many times this happens, she will do it over and over again.

When I have my bath robe on, I'll wrap the sleeve around my hand and play with her because she seems to enjoy quite rough games. If I don't cover my hand and arm I will get scratched and bitten quite badly.

When we play fight Coco will stop every few minutes and do the lying down kicking herself antics. It looks like it must hurt but she doesn't seem to mind. Also, every evening around dinner time, she runs laps round and round the house. She gallops quickly through all the rooms and then flops down on the living room rug for a rest.

Polly and Molly
Laura, 15

We got Polly when I was four, the year I joined school after leaving the nursery. She's a beautiful tabby cat who has a huge appetite. She eventually became so obese that her stomach would drag across the floor. We took her to the vet who did some tests. He put her on a special diet and she has lost a lot of weight. Now I call her my "skinny minny" and she's no longer a fat cat (although she isn't exactly thin either). She constantly tries to escape from her diet by stealing food out of the rubbish bin or begging from the neighbours. She's so sneaky when she's up to something. We had to tell the neighbours about her condition to stop them feeding her and they've been really good about it.

Our other cat, Molly, was brought home by my mum who found her near where she works. Molly was obviously a stray; she was starving hungry and very thin and scruffy so my mum brought her home to live with us. She was really bony but now she has taken Polly's place as the fattest cat of the house. She seems very proud of her big stomach and spends a lot of time washing it.

Betty the Nutcase
Dinah, 30

Our four-year-old black and white cat, Betty, has been given the nickname Nutcase because of her loopy behaviour.

She's extremely curious and has to check out everything that I am eating. Sometimes she'll let me know how she feels about it as well. She's decided eggs or omelette is something that she doesn't like, so, if I eat anything with eggs in it and she smells it, she'll pull her head back, put her ears down and run off.

She's also pretty silly when it comes to water. When she was first checking out the flat, she got curious as to what I was doing at the sink. She jumped up on the counter to investigate and ended up covered in water and soap suds. She just sat there watching me, it didn't bother her. However, if you spray her with a water bottle, you will get a completely different reaction. She'll run to get away from the spraying and then give you a look as if she's trying to make you feel as bad as she possibly can for doing it. Yet if you soak her with water from the washing up bowl, she doesn't react.

She also clearly feels that I shouldn't sleep for too long. She's got a method to wake me. First, she'll crawl up onto my legs and walk up my back (I generally sleep on my stomach), then she'll meow in my ear. If I don't respond she'll turn and start to knead on my back. I call it a massage. If that doesn't work she'll climb onto my pillow and stare at me right in the face. If I sense her there and open my eyes, she'll let out this loud meow and start purring. If I close my eyes again, she leans in and licks my nose. If that doesn't work, she'll bite my nose. That generally gets a reaction from me. I'll either get up as she prances around the bed, rejoicing the fact that she's won or I'll roll over causing her to start the entire process all over again.

She hates it when we go out and leave her alone in the house. We always get an angry meow when we return home. We give her filtered water to drink and she absolutely loves it. She'll keep drinking if you refill her bowl and she does one of three things after drinking the water. If it's freshly cold, she acts as if it's an energy drink. She'll drink some and then race around the flat, jumping over furniture and knocking as much over as she can. Other times, she'll look straight up to the ceiling after drinking and give a gargle-like meow. Sometimes she does a whole body shake after drinking as if she's just had a hard work-out class.

Her favourite food is salmon. She gives out a loud "Now!" when we get her salmon-flavoured treats out, and walks up and down the kitchen on her back legs, pawing at the air. She also gets obsessive when it comes to hunting down bugs. Even after they're long gone or she's caught and eaten the bug, she'll still look around for more. It's really funny to watch her attempt to catch a bug with two paws; when she misses she lets out this meow that sounds like "Damn it!" She attacks her own tail and steals bread, buns and crackers if she gets the chance.

Her latest trick is to sit on the back of the toilet. She'll meow a hello if you walk by the bathroom and she's in there. I've taken to keeping the lid shut because I'm afraid that she might fall into it. In general, she's the nuttiest cat I've ever met.

Morning Calls
Rachel, 47

I've never been very good at getting up in the mornings.

However, every cat I've ever owned has done whatever it takes to wake me up to get their breakfast. I had one cat called Gertie who used to throw herself at the mirror-fronted built-in wardrobes. The sound of the glass shaking would have me sitting bolt upright in bed immediately.

Another one, called Jim, found a way to get into the storage drawers under my bed and I'd wake up to rustling and scrabbling underneath me. It was a very strange way to wake me up, but it worked every time.

Once I even took in a stray cat that would sit underneath my bedroom window and howl until I got up and gave her some food. I suppose it was my fault for having fed her in the first place.

Monty and the Beetle
Joe, 46

I have two cats, Monty and Pinky. The other day as I was making lunch in the kitchen I heard the sound of a cat choking. Pinky was by the kitchen door looking worried, twitching her ears about so I immediately knew that something was wrong with Monty. He was outside staggering around coughing and hacking. Then he stopped coughing and walked over to an old flower pot outside that has some rain water in it. He stuck his head in it again and then the coughing and spluttering returned. I had to go over to see what was going on.

Inside the flower pot there was about two inches of water and swimming around in it was a large beetle. It was the beetle that had grabbed Monty's attention. He kept trying to get at the beetle with his mouth, getting water up his nose then performing the whole spluttering act.

I was actually quite relieved that there was nothing seriously wrong; I'd been worrying that he might have swallowed a pebble or something. As I watched him trying to get the drowned bug I couldn't help laughing. Every time the sneezing subsided, he went straight back and put his nose into the water again. He carried on this way for about ten minutes until my sides were aching with laughter and I had to stop him.

I went over to the flower pot and tipped the water out. The bug fell onto the patio and Monty pounced on it. He gave it a couple of chews and then spat it out in disgust, and it crawled away unharmed. He'd been drowning himself all afternoon for nothing.

Leo the Lion
Zoe, 27

Our cat Leo is like a big lion. He's a huge tabby cat and the stripes on his side actually look very like a tiger's stripes. He has a strange personality. He likes to lie on me when I'm lounging on the sofa and if I stroke the bridge of his nose and over toward the back of his head with my finger, he will open his mouth and keep it open. He looks like he's giving me a big grin. It's actually the start of a yawn. If I do it enough, he will yawn every time. But it's the grin that is so funny.

Leo definitely has a unique personality. He curls up on my lap when I'm on the computer. When I start typing, he puts his paw over my arm and starts nibbling his toes. When I scratch the top of his head, he always purrs. He doesn't only meow, he grunts a lot too. He washes his sister Lucy's face and head in a very loving way. He hops in the bath sometimes and attacks the shower curtain. When I scratch my face he gently bites my arm as if he thinks I'm hurting myself. He's very comforting.

Sometimes I hear Leo scrabbling around in the kitchen and I know that he's up to no good. He knocks things off shelves so that they fall on the floor. If I pick it up and put it on the table, and tap him lightly on the head, he does it again as soon as my back's turned. I walk away and I hear a crash as something else falls to the floor.

I do love him though. There's never a dull moment when he's around.

Suzie and Frank
Belinda, 38

I have two cats. My female cat, Suzie, wakes me up at the same time every morning by walking all over the bed and on top of me, chirping like a bird. She has to follow me into the bathroom every morning and drink out of the tap whilst I brush my teeth. She also likes to grab at the toilet paper to get it to unravel. Instead of lapping up water from her bowl with her tongue, she will dip her paw in the water and lick it off that. She also likes to chew on anything plastic. She especially loves those plastic strips they use to seal the lids on tubs of margarine or ice cream. Those are her favourite; she chews on them until they're full of holes. Suzie also likes to hide in cupboards. I had to put a child safety latch on the ones under the kitchen and bathroom sinks to keep her away from the cleaning sprays. Even so, I still hear the banging of the cupboard door slamming shut while she tries to paw it open.

Frank, my male cat has an obsession with ice-cream and egg mayonnaise. If you try to eat either of those things he will pester and pester you until you give him some. He also pushes at the water bowl before he drinks from it as if that's the only way he can tell that there's something in it. He has occasionally dragged the water bowl all over the kitchen. I ended up buying an extra heavy one meant for dogs so that he couldn't move it so easily. He also walks across my computer keyboard and occasionally lies down and goes to sleep on it so that I can't work. Frank is the cuddlier of the two though; he loves to touch noses with you and give you 'kisses'.

Curiosity and the Cat
Debbie, 31

Domino is a big furry, gentle male cat, who has become part of our household. He used to be a feral cat, and we started feeding him at the back door but gradually he started coming into the house. He eventually became quite socialised and would be in the house sometimes for hours at a time. He would find his perfect place in the sun on a comfy cushion and fall asleep. He also liked to follow me around, head-butting my leg. I would stroke him until he indicated he was tired of the game and wanted to sleep, or eat, or groom.

One day, I had to tidy and organise some things in the basement. We tend to put all our junk down there because I'm not very good at throwing things away. I forgot that Domino was in the house. The next thing I saw was Domino on the stairs, sniffing the air and preparing to explore a bit of the house that he hadn't ever seen before. I didn't really want him poking around down there because there are many ways in which he could get himself injured or trapped so I walked towards him speaking gently and hoping to persuade him to go back upstairs.

I think I succeeded only in scaring him because he bolted for a dark corner of the room. I think he might have been looking for another way out but as he scrambled up a pile of furniture, he spotted the door of an old mahogany chest that was slightly open and he charged inside. I'm not sure how it happened, but something about his sudden movements inside it tipped the chest over, shutting the door on the underside and trapping Domino inside, and a couple of old chairs then slid off a pile behind it; the noise it all made was as if a ten tonne truck had crashed into the building.

I panicked and ran to the heap of furniture calling Domino's name. I heard him making angry meows as if I'd trapped him. He didn't sound hurt, just very annoyed.

I pulled the chairs away but I was worried about moving the chest; it was too heavy and I was worried about dropping it on him if I lifted it up to let him out. I had to go next door and find my neighbour to help me.

John, my next door neighbour is an ex-police officer and since retiring has kept himself fit. When I explained to him what had happened, he came over immediately and between the two of us we carefully lifted the chest up again.

I opened the door carefully to find a furious feline face glaring out at me from the gloom of the dusty old wood. He shot out through the door and ran upstairs and outside. I didn't see him at all for a couple of days but he did eventually come back and enjoy home comforts once again.

He eventually moved in for good but he's never again gone down into the basement.

Girl or Boy?
Faye, 32

When we moved to the country my daughter begged us to get her a cat. Luckily, we found a nearby family with kittens for sale and drove over to their house to pick a kitten. They had two grey tabby kittens left, one male and one female - we chose the tiny female. My daughter was very happy and called her Susu.

A couple of days later, we took Susu to the vet for a general check-up. The vet examined Susu and then politely informed us that Susu was in fact a male kitten. We couldn't stop laughing, but we decided to keep his name because we'd all got used to calling him Susu.

Susu has been the greatest cat, he was extremely playful as a kitten and loved to play football with a ping pong ball, chasing it round and round and guarding it if you tried to take it off him. Sometimes we'd take a piece of tinfoil, screw it up into a ball, and then throw it across the room. He loved to chase things. He would bat it around and back to you, like he was playing a football match.

Another strong personality trait he had was that he loved to climb. I was woken early one morning by a strange noise, only to find him clinging to the top of the curtains. About ten seconds later the whole curtain plus curtain rail fell to the floor. Susu was nowhere to be seen. Then he appeared on the other side of the bed looking at me as if saying, "It was nothing to do with me".

He also liked to sit on top of the door to any room watching people going in and out. Occasionally he would reach out to bat someone's head with his paw and then form a crouching attack position to challenge you to attack back.

I often used to find him tucked up in bed with my daughter when I went into her room to switch off her reading lamp.

He'd just give a little yawn noise and then settle back down to sleep.

He's about seven years old now but he hasn't mellowed much. He's scampering around the house and playful as ever.

Crazy Cat
Gaynor, 35

On my last birthday, some of my friends got me a female cat called Hattie. She was a lovely tortoiseshell cat with very pronounced stripes. She loved to play with the feather duster and was very dainty and dignified.

When Hattie was about four months old I decided to take her to the vet to have her spayed and was given the news that Hattie was actually a male! The vet explained that of all the millions of tortoiseshell cats born very year only a very few are born male. Basically, I had a torty-tom cat. I don't know why I didn't notice. I just assumed that all tortoiseshell cats were female because that was what I had been told.

I re-named Hattie Hal, and had him neutered to stop him wandering off. It was strange getting used to the fact that he was a boy. He was still the same cat but I began to have different expectations of him. However, he wasn't prepared to change; he still loved the feather duster and he loved to sit on my lap.

Another thing that Hal absolutely loved to do was to sit in the bath, (without water in it). Everyday when I came home from work I would find Hal sitting in the middle of the bath tub, giving me a look that was a little challenging, as if to say "Who are you to tell me what to do?" I used to wonder what would happen if I filled that bath with water before I left for work.

Hal also used to dash into the shower whilst it was running and make a fuss because he was getting wet, then take a swipe at me for getting him wet. Cats can be very stupid.

Nowadays, Hal likes to spend most of his time stalking around the house on his search and destroy missions. Newspapers, flowers and slippers don't stand a chance. They are chewed, shredded and discarded with disdain.

I may spend a lot of time making fun of Hal, but I really should mention how sweet he is. He's very friendly, even with other cats, who often respond to his greetings with a swipe from an outstretched claw. He also loves people and can often be found on the wall outside our house meowing at anyone who will listen. I sit at our window sometimes watching him and it is amazing how many people stop to say hello to him and to make a fuss of him.

Tula's Habits
Lara, 30

I have a one-year-old cat called Tula and she has a weird habit of licking my hair. She climbs onto my lap and then crawls up to my shoulder and begins her licking. I think that she thinks she is giving me a wash but I always end up having to wash my hair because it smells of cat food.

Occasionally she attacks my head and bites and grabs at my scalp which really hurts. Then she just goes back to licking. She pulls my hair to wake me up in the morning. I have tried different shampoos in case that's what she likes but it didn't make any difference.

Bodkin and the Bubbles
Julia, 25

I have a cat called Bodkin who loves to be in the bathroom with me whilst I have my bath. I always put a lot of bubble bath in when I want to have a long soak and Bodkin thinks it's hilarious. I lie low in the water and blow bubbles at him with my hand. He always gets excited with huge black pupils and puffed up whiskers. Then, he jumps onto the side of the bath and starts walking round it purring all the time. Sometimes he starts tapping at the bubbles with his paws, looking bewildered when they pop and disappear in front of him.

One day he got a bit too frisky and actually fell into the bath. It was as if it happened in slow motion. I could see the look on his little face as his feet slipped on the sides of the bath, then there was a huge splash, surprisingly huge for such a little animal and Bodkin was in the bath with me. His head popped up out of the water covered in bubbles then he jumped out of the bath and raced off leaving the air full of bubbles floating after him.

Since then he's much more careful at bath time. When I have a soak, he watches me from a distance.

Wildlife Lover
Leah, 26

I have a cat called Angel that watches TV. She absolutely loves wildlife documentaries. She will start by watching the TV from wherever she is and as the programme progresses, she will move closer to the TV until she ends up sitting in front of it. It has got to the point where we daren't change the channel if anything about animals and birds comes on because she's instantly hooked when she sees and hears the animals on TV.

We were watching a documentary about the Arctic the other day and she was enjoying watching the polar bears. She jumped up on the TV table and sat right in front of the screen, following the animals as they wandered through the snow. When she was a kitten we were watching a programme about wolves and, when they began to howl, she hid behind the sofa. I think now she's fully grown she wants to get into the television to get her own back on the wolves that scared her.

Striper and Boots

Karen, 20

I have loved cats for as long as I can remember. When I was little, I wanted a pet lion but when I was told that that wouldn't be possible I settled for the common or garden house cat.

My first pet cat was a big, black and white fluffy cat called Cotton. He was quite old when I was born; I think he died when I was about three. I only vaguely remember him; I was always following this enormous long-haired creature about. I can remember that he was about the same size as me.

When I was about five we got a new cat. This one I do remember. She was a grey tabby cat with an enormous pair of ears on her little stripy head. We took her home when she was 12 weeks old. Mum asked me what I wanted to call her and I came up with Striper because I liked the pattern of her stripes. From then on she was absolutely my cat and I think my mum didn't get enough of a chance to play with Striper because a few months later, we saw an advertisement in the local newspaper for a good home needed for a kitten, and we decided to get another one.

Our new kitten was also stripy but brown rather than grey and it was a boy kitten that seemed to be very sociable. He had been found alone by the side of the road. All four of his paws were black and the rest of him was brown tabby. We took him home and called him Boots.

I grew up with Striper and Boots and they are like family to me. Striper used to sleep on my bed and Boots would stay in my mum's bed. Striper loved to sleep on my pillow although if mum caught her she would make me push her to the bottom of the bed. Striper and Boots became great friends and played at chasing each other around the house and garden. Boots was very greedy and Striper was full of mischief. She would know when my mum put the cat food down and she would hide behind the washing machine and pounce on Boots as soon as he got his head down in his bowl. No matter how many times she did it, his eagerness to eat meant that he was never prepared and would let out a loud squawk.

Both cats are quite old now but they're still playful, if a little slower than they were. I've left home now and go to college and they still make a fuss of me when I go home for visits. I don't want to think about how long I have left with them, they mean so much to me.

Melons
Diane, 28

My cat absolutely loves melons. She's a tabby and white cat called Bella, and I've never met a cat who was so obsessed with anything in the way that Bella is obsessed with melons. It doesn't matter what type of melon I buy. If I happened to have brought a cantaloupe, a water melon or a honeydew melon home from grocery shopping, Bella will be in the kitchen in a heartbeat. It's like she just sniffs them out.

I set the poor innocent piece of fruit on the counter and my cat will attack it. I'm not talking a few nibbles; she bashes it around and takes huge chunks from it. I'm not sure how much of it she actually eats – she takes these funny bites then shakes her head and it ends up in pieces on the floor. If we actually want to eat a melon, we have to put it in a closed container so she can't get it. We once accidentally left one out overnight and it was pretty much destroyed by the morning. She's absolutely ridiculous.

The Hat Thief
Mark, 33

I have known very few cats that I don't love. I have always shared my food with them and my bed and sofa too. My favourite at the moment is my Mikey, he follows me everywhere and is into everything I am. He even plays around with the soap suds when I wash my car. Strangely enough he loves to play in the shower too. He stands outside the curtain waiting his turn and jumps into the puddle of water just as I'm getting out; he often just sits in the draining water and licks his paws. He once charged in there with me and didn't seem to mind getting soaked. He sits next to my sink, watching, when I brush my teeth or shave.

The other day he stole my hat when I was working in the garden and wouldn't give it back without a fight. He had his teeth into it, all of his claws in it, eyes narrowed, ears back, and he was kicking and slapping my hand every time I reached for it. In the end, I offered him some cat biscuits which were just about enough to get my hat back. He ran off with my socks this morning whilst I was in the shower.

He's a nuisance but an adorable nuisance.

Misty
Jane, 30

I have a half-Persian cat called Misty and she is a really sweet princess. She chases my feet under the bed covers if I try to move and sometimes gently bites and pulls my hair when I'm asleep.

Misty loves children. When my sister brings my two-year-old nephew and three-year-old niece over, Misty trots everywhere after them and loves to play with them both. It's always surprised me because most cats flee in terror from any nearby children.

Misty is naughty in the kitchen though, because she is always trying to get onto the worktops when I'm cooking. If I don't give her a treat I often get a quick nip on the ankle. She really loves her food and gets very grumpy if I don't share my salmon or chicken with her.

Oh, and I am never allowed to eat ice-cream in peace unless I give her a bowl too.

The Music Critic
Carol, 27

My cat Dylan is an absolute darling except for one thing. He hates me singing. If I'm singing along to the radio in the kitchen he will run in and start attacking me. He turns into a snarling little beast at the sound of my voice.

It started when he was a kitten. He's a little tabby cat and from the day I got him he was always very cuddly. We would curl up together on the sofa and he would stretch out and purr contentedly. Then, one day I was in the kitchen preparing dinner and singing along to some song that was on the radio when Dylan came rushing into the kitchen and sank his teeth into my leg. At first I thought he was being playful and gently pushed him away. He sat down on the kitchen floor staring at me. I went back to my cooking and started singing again. He hissed and snarled and went for my legs again. It happened every time I started singing.

Of course back then it wasn't too bad because he was only a tiny kitten but now he's a chubby two year old and the attacks are more painful. I have given up singing in the kitchen but I still like to sing in the shower. I lock the bathroom door so that he can't get at me and when I come out of the bathroom he's sitting outside the door looking furious.

There was one time when I didn't lock the bathroom door and Dylan got in. I was happily singing and showering when I felt something huge leap at me from the other side of the shower curtain. As I fought to get out of the shower, Dylan pulled the entire shower curtain and rail into the bath and landed in a ball of fury. Then of course he also got wet which is something he hates and after scratching my foot he fled out of the room.

After I had got dressed, I went down to the kitchen and Dylan was back to his cuddly self as if nothing had happened. He rubbed around my legs purring and wanting food. He just can't stand me singing.

Over the Wall
Mark, 32

My cat Bobo is a bit stupid; he loves to jump out of windows. It doesn't matter what floor of the house he's on, he always goes straight out of the window if I leave it open. Because of this, I normally make sure the upstairs windows are closed but last summer during a very hot night I had to leave my bedroom window open.

I woke up an hour after going to bed and realised that Bobo wasn't in my room. With a sinking feeling I put my head out of the window and called for him. I could hear him meowing his head off, but I had no idea where he could be. I leaned out of the window as far as I could and I could just about tell that the sound was coming from the high wall that separates my garden from my neighbours. He must have jumped out of the window onto the tall wall outside and then down to the ground in my neighbours garden. Resigned to Bobo's stupidity, I put on my dressing gown and went downstairs to get him.

I went into the garden and hoisted myself up the wall by standing on a large terracotta pot. Fortunately, Bobo was sitting on the other side of the wall but it was too high for me to climb over to get him. I encouraged him to jump up the wall so I could catch him. He tried once, but the wall was too high and after that failure he refused to try again. I was leaning over the wall for over half an hour calling him and patting the wall, but he was stubborn and wouldn't budge; he just carried on his pitiful meowing. He did attempt to climb up the wall by just walking but obviously that didn't work. I decided that I had to get something to put over the other side of the wall to help him reach up it.

In the process of me climbing down from the wall to try and solve this predicament, the pot beneath me fell over and I smacked my head against the wall. I tried placing a pole over the other side diagonally so he could walk on it, but he clearly had no clue what it was for and just sat there twitching his ears in the way cats do when they're confused. So, I resorted to climbing back down the wall, going back in the house for the garage keys and getting the expandable ladders from the back of the garage.

I put the ladders against the wall and climbed to the top. I had to sit balancing on the top of the wall to pull up the ladders and then lower them down the other side. I encouraged Bobo to climb up them but he still sat there looking dumb so I climbed down into my neighbour's garden, picked up the cat and climbed back to the top of the wall. After I had brought the ladders over the wall again Bobo seemed to have got the idea and instantly climbed down them back into our garden. I struggled down in my dressing gown.

Back inside Bobo went straight to his food bowl and kicked up a fuss. It was by then about 3am and I had been outside for about an hour. I refused to reward my stupid cat with food for such foolish behaviour and went straight upstairs to bed. I fell asleep to his meows of protest.

I woke up the next morning with several cuts and bruises on my legs and quite a sore arm. My cat is a very lucky one, I tell you.

Feline Inebriated
Tim, 37

I have a cat called Sandy; he's a lovely Abyssinian cat with sandy-red coloured fur. One night I discovered that Sandy has a taste for red wine. I was sitting watching TV with a glass of wine when I heard a slurping sound. I looked down and Sandy had his face in my wine glass licking up the drink! Soon afterwards, he began to walk around the living room bumping into things and shouting out his loud 'wah' noise. Then he came up to me, bit my arm and fell over sideways before rolling over onto his back with his paws in the air purring. I realised my cat was drunk.

I tried to call him into the kitchen thinking that giving him some food might be helpful. He trotted in and then spent half an hour lying in the sink drinking the drip of water that came out of the tap. Whenever I went over to stroke him and make sure that he was OK, he bit my arm gently and made his funny wah noise. I fed him some cat biscuits as he lay in the sink to soak up the alcohol and he munched them gratefully. Eventually he went to sleep.

The next day he was back to normal although a little subdued at breakfast. It hasn't stopped him trying for my wine again though. I have to put it out of his reach or he'll have some. Maybe he enjoyed being drunk.

The Secret Cat
Ruby, 15

My cat is called Yoyo. When I first got him my parents didn't know about him as I was trying to hide him from them in my bedroom. I kept him in a drawer and used to sneak bits of food upstairs to him. A few weeks later I had an invitation to stay at a friend's house for the weekend so I took my brother to meet Yoyo and he agreed to feed him for me whilst I was away.

I think Yoyo must have missed me because he started meowing and my mum went into my room and found him. My brother telephoned me to tell me and I was so worried that she might make me get rid of him.

I was in trouble, of course. But luckily, he grew on her, and she loves him to death now. He is such a charming cat. He's very loyal and loving; sometimes he seems more like a dog than a cat. I'm just so happy that he worked his magic on my mum and so I was allowed to keep him.

The Sunday Roast
Janice, 38

Last year we bought two little Siamese kittens, one male and one female. The male was quite a large kitten and we called him Samson. The female was a tiny little thing with dainty little paws. We called her Delilah.

The first weekend we had them we cooked roast beef for supper. After the food was served up we put the rest of the meat joint on the worktop in the kitchen and sat down to eat. As we were eating our daughter asked for a cup of juice and I went into the kitchen to get it for her. I couldn't believe what I saw.

Delilah had climbed up onto the worktop and had the joint of meat in her teeth. She was so tiny it was the same size as her. I immediately tried to pick her up and take her away from the meat but when I did she still held fast to the roast beef with her teeth. For a tiny kitten she had very powerful jaws.

I took her into the dining room (still hanging off the meat she was holding in her mouth), to show my husband and daughter what I had found. She even growled when we tried to take it off her. I eventually got it out of her mouth and was surprised to find that the meat was actually quite a lot heavier than the cat!

Now if we have Sunday roasts we have to put the joint of meat on top of the kitchen cupboards where she can't get at it.

Noir the Noisy Cat
Helena, 28

Our cat is called Noir because he is a deep glossy black. He often does strange things such as stick his head inside your shoes or dangle from the curtain rails. He will only drink water from a cup not a bowl and when you go to bed he gets into it under the covers with you. He also loves dog food.

Our three year old daughter calls him Noise which is very funny because he is a very vocal and loud cat. He has also begun to warn me before I get a migraine. He will climb onto my shoulder and sit there purring about five minutes before the attack comes on. This means that I can take my medication to ease the pain before it develops.

My First Cat
Hal, 39

The first cat we ever had was a tabby called Benny. We had bought a plot of land and were building a house on it at the weekends. Once we had built the main shell of the house and were fixing up the interior, we took Benny with us so that he would get used to the house and the area. It was when we were finishing the kitchen that we lost him.

It was quite late at night then, probably after 10pm because it was dark out. We could hear a feint meow now and again but as we wandered from room to room there was no sign of Benny. The rooms were empty at that point so there was no furniture that he could have hidden behind, but he was definitely somewhere in the house.

We called his name and the answering meows were much stronger in the kitchen. That day we had finished putting in a row of cupboards along one wall and at the back of one cupboard was a gap between the cupboard and the wall. Benny must have somehow got himself into that space without our noticing. There was nothing for it, the cupboard would have to be removed.

I unscrewed it from the wall but it seemed that the cat had got into the wall cavity and it would be a much harder job than we first thought to get Benny to safety. We tried to coax him to come back through the hole in the wall but he looked suspicious and carried on meowing. In the end we had to cut a hole in the wall so that we could pull our cat free.

We lifted Benny to safety and he was purring and very happy if a little dusty. When we finally moved into that house Benny spent a long time refusing to go into the kitchen.

Under the Covers
Kate, 29

I have two cats from different litters and they are both very lovable in their own ways. Buck, is a large black cat with long spiky fur. He loves to come in and snuggle with me at night. The only problem is that he is so big that when he sits on me in the night it feels as if I have been pinned to the bed with bricks. He usually spends the bulk of the night on my bed. In fact, the only time that he's not asleep, he is eating.

My female cat Linka, is a slinky, slim chocolate point Siamese and loves to sleep under the covers with me. Sometimes however, Buck gets very jealous and attacks her under the covers as if there's a large mouse under the carpet. On those nights I get little sleep! It's best if Linka comes in very early in the morning and sneaks into the bed when Buck's not looking or when I'm having a nap.

Pitta Lover
Sam, 20

I have a cat called Casey who is mad about pitta bread. Whenever anyone takes a pack of pitta bread out of the freezer so that it can thaw, Casey will jump onto the table and start to attack the plastic wrapping with his teeth. If he succeeds in getting some bread out he will run off and eat it quickly as if it is his favourite treat in the world. Sometimes, he doesn't even wait for it to thaw slightly.

My sister and I tried a little experiment, and put out a plate with ham and chicken on the table and then put out another plate with pitta bread on it.

Unbelievably, Casey went for the pitta bread! He also likes green olives but does a strange thing with them. Before eating them he rubs her chin over and over them as if they're covered with catnip. Then he chews them for a while before leaving them on the floor. I think he likes the salty liquid they are often kept in, but doesn't really like the taste once he has licked the salt off.

Bobsy and the Alarm Clock
David, 22

My cat Bobsy attacks my alarm clock every morning. Without fail, my alarm clock beeps and then there is a cacophony of yowls as Bobsy tries to kill it before I can switch it off. Even if I shut him out of my bedroom, as soon as he hears it go off he attacks my bedroom door then, when I open the door, comes in and attacks my alarm clock for having rung without him there to stop it. I have tried all different kinds of clocks, radio ones set to a talk show or music show, electronic ones, even my mobile phone; it doesn't matter, Bobsy is after them all. He often fools me into a false sense of security by hiding under the bed where I can't see him and then leaping out at the first sound from the bedside table.

Someone once suggested that I not set the alarm and let Bobsy wake me instead. I tried that and didn't wake until 10.30am. Bobsy was still peacefully snoozing at the bottom of my bed. I nearly got sacked from my job, after trying to explain my cat trouble to my boss. It seems that Bobsy is just angry with the noise in the mornings, he'd rather sleep.

So would I really, but someone has to pay for the cat food.

Puddles, Sweetie and Coco
Heidi, 30

I used to suffer from depression but now I have cats and they make me smile everyday. I have three called Puddles, Sweetie and Coco. I have had Puddles for over two years and he is my charming young man. Puddles brightens my mood no matter what, he is the most lovable cat ever. I called him Puddles because whenever it rained he went straight outside and came back all muddy, meowing to be dried in a soft towel. Sweetie is my chubby girl; she is about eighteen months old and doesn't care about anything except food and getting cuddles. Coco is a brave independent young lady who is still only four months old. She attacks anything that moves and is very ambitious about going out exploring in her own. I sometimes worry that she's got lost but she always comes home eventually.

Crazy about Cats

Many cat lovers would describe themselves as being crazy about cats, but some pet owners stand out as being especially affectionate in their approach to the feline world!

Bruce the Chatty Cat
Susan, 58

I'm one of those crazy cat people. I have one cat called Bruce and he means the world to me. I adopted him as a stray when he was about eight months old. I often tell people that I prefer his company to the company of most people. He's a very verbal cat (half Siamese) and so he talks all the time. I talk back to him. I know we're not really having conversations (I'm not that nuts), but it looks like we are. I also talk to him out loud a lot.

I live alone and it gets lonely sometimes. I like talking to Bruce because he doesn't care what I talk about or how much I complain or how often I repeat the same story over and over. He's a trouble maker and can make me furious at times by destroying things, tearing up newspapers, jumping on anything that will hold still, randomly biting me, etc. but all he has to do is give me those eyes and I'm back to cuddling him and calling him my baby. He's very spoiled. He sleeps with me and sits on me most of the time. He has tons of toys. He lets me rock him and snuggle him (though it's only for as long as he wants). He's really wonderful company. I think he's the best cat in the world.

Princess
Karina, 27

I have a cat called Princess and I love her as if she were my daughter. And yes, she is really spoilt, probably more than I would spoil a child. Princess however, gets whatever she wants. She even has her own chair at the dinner table.

It's interesting how we communicate with each other. Princess understands what I'm saying by the tone of my voice and I understand what she wants by her body language and how she meows. When she's hungry she uses a low tone and says "mow" but when she wants to play, it's more of an upbeat cry that sounds like "meeoww".

Street Entertainers
Iris, 40

I consider all cats as my cat because I absolutely adore cats and simply can't pass one in the street without stopping for a chat. My husband has asthma so I can't have cats in my house but I greet and even sometimes feed cats that turn up in my garden. Cats are such entertainers; they are by far the funniest animal in the world. Every time I see a cat, it brings a smile on my face. I know you'll think I'm mad but when nobody's watching, I talk to them in my own made up language.

Six Cats
Gary, 49

I lost one of my legs in a motorbike accident some years ago and I live with my sister as my carer. I had one cat before my accident and then when I came to live with my sister she already had three. You'd think that four cats would be enough but we're both committed cat lovers.

Last winter we found two stray cats living in our basement. We were concerned because the weather was really cold. We took them some food and made sure that they had plenty of unfrozen water. Eventually they both appeared at our kitchen door; clearly we had pleased them too much. They were both females and the first thing we did was take them to be spayed, I think six cats is enough even for us!

Missy and Mister
Tina, 22

I just adore my cats. I have two called Missy and Mister. They are both ginger stripy cats and I love them to death. I often feel like life would not be complete without my little darlings. They are like my children; I don't actually want any kids. With my cats I don't need an alarm clock. Missy and Mister wake me up every morning at the same time. Mister rubs my ears to get my attention so that I will get up and go and put some food in their bowls. After I've had a hard day, their affection and their purring calms me, and their love is as unconditional as my love for them.

Lulu
Alice, 66

My cat, Lulu, is really spoiled. I wouldn't spoil a child like that or it would grow up selfish and demanding, but Lulu gets whatever she wants. She even has her own chair at the table and her own plate there where I put her portion of food.

It's interesting that we can communicate with each other. Other people think that I'm mad but I don't think I am. I just love my cat.

The Menagerie
Corrine. 41

I'm a huge cat lover. Over the past twenty years I have never been without one, there was a time when I had six after keeping the kittens that my eldest cat had. They have all had their own personalities. They were naughty and playful or angry and stubborn, one was scared of plastic bags and another was very bossy. All of them were independent and I think they are more loyal and loving than dogs.

At the moment I have a dog, two cats, a parrot, three budgies and a baby rat. Strangely enough they all get along together. The only issue is that one of my cats keeps eating the dog's food and he daren't push her out of the way.

My Best Friend
Gina, 23

When I was eight years old I came home from school to find that my mum had got me a kitten. She had got him from a rescue centre and he was about two months old. I called him Smokey. He has bluey-grey fur and bright green eyes and I instantly fell in love with him.

There have been times when I think I've loved Smokey more than my actual family. He's always been like my best friend and I think that he knows me better than anyone else. Whenever I was having a bad time at school he would lie on my bed next to me and purr. When I'm upset he crawls in next to me and I can whisper to him about why I'm sad. He's just such a comfort to me. Smokey's a great listener and always talks back to you. He doesn't really meow, he shouts. He's so funny; it's impossible not to laugh with him around. He's the most lovable cat in the world and loves to sit on everyone's lap and be stroked.

Everyone makes fun of me for my love for Smokey. I treat him like he's my baby. But just as Smokey relies on me to feed him, give him water and cuddles, I think I also rely on him. Smokey is now fifteen years old and I'm twenty-three, but I'm still the little girl I used to be when I'm with my cat. As for Smokey, his grey coat is duller than it used to be and his hips have become bony. I still hug him close every night. The thought of him dying always makes me cry and I think about it a lot since he is now so old. The thought of being without him upsets me so much. He's been my constant companion for most of my life. I know I'll never be able to replace him.

Muffin
Gill, 29

I love my cat, Muffin. She's called Muffin because she looks a bit top heavy, just like a muffin. She's mostly brown in colour and she has a very large, solid head and body and little puny legs.

She is an excellent hunter, especially of human food; she always finds a way to grab a piece of chicken or other food out of my hand. She is a wonderful conversationalist, whatever I say, she always meows her opinion back to me. I never get the last word.

I also never get the most comfortable spot on the sofa, the sunniest spot in the garden or the last piece of fish. It's funny how we put up with traits in animals that we would never tolerate in another human!

My Cat Cindy
Daniel, 37

We are quite a big family and really, in my house, there are six cats, but each person seems to have picked their own. Luckily the cat I chose, Cindy, also chose me and we're inseparable. Cindy's the most amazing cat; I love her almost as if she were my daughter. She really has a special bond with me; she even gets jealous if I spend too much time with any of the other cats.

She always cuddles up to me on my bed, and falls asleep next to me at night. In the morning, if I wake up late, she's downstairs meowing as if she's looking for me. Then she'll come up to my room and meow at me to get up. If I don't get up immediately I get bitten, but they're playful bites. She'll sniff my arm and then next thing you know, bite it, then dance away to see how I react. She's such an odd cat. When she was younger she'd always jump on my back and I ended up with a lot of scratches. Whilst she was on my back I'd have to take her for rides up and down the stairs and through the house. As she's got older though, she doesn't do that so much which is good because she's quite heavy and chunky these days.

Toby the Bengal Cat
Debbie, 34

I love cats and I always have. I have five of them in my home. This spring I got an eight-week-old Bengal cat that is absolutely unique, completely different from any cat I have ever had. He is extremely affectionate, hysterically funny, very loyal, and has quite a personality. He loves to jump high in the air to try to catch those cat toys that are feathers on the end of a stick and cloth rope.

Toby steals our socks and acts as if we should be very proud of him for catching a wild mouse. He loves to sleep in the laundry basket when it's full of clean clothes waiting to be ironed. When I sort the laundry out, he flings himself into the pile and buries himself happily, like a child jumping around in a pile of leaves. It's just the same when I make the beds; he throws himself onto the bed and tunnels under the duvet cover. When I eventually get the cover off the duvet, he then pounces onto the mattress so that I can't put a fresh sheet on it. It probably takes about twenty minutes longer now to change the bedding than it did before I got him, but it definitely makes it more fun. I have read that Bengal cats are more like dogs in their friendliness and loyalty to their human companions and considering Toby, I think this is probably true.

He is also a real comedian. He will leap onto the back of the sofa only to slide down the other side on his back. He keeps trying to get into the drawers under my bed by making a sprint for them whenever they're open. He did manage to get into a drawer once and from there crept underneath the bed. I had to take out the entire drawer to get him back. There's never a dull moment with him.

Toby has also demonstrated to me that cats do not need ladders to reach picture rails, they just climb the wallpaper. He loves water so I've introduced 'bath night' for him. On his bath nights he greets the shallow water with joy then chases rubber ducks around for about an hour.

Throw a ball, a roll of paper or a mouse toy and it will be retrieved and placed at your feet to be thrown again. If you ignore him Toby responds by doing a rugby tackle around your legs with all four paws.

Usually I don't like animals sharing my bed, probably because I have so many cats, but after several sleepless nights where Toby tried to tear up the carpet outside the bedroom door, Toby now sleeps at the bottom of the bed on his own blanket. I wouldn't be surprised if, by the time winter arrives, I wake up to find a furry lump snuggled up to me under the covers.

Sometimes I feel as if I've got an extra ten cats rather than just one but I'm so glad I got him.

The Not-So Empty Nest
Brenda, 72

I have had four children and now they are all grown up and have left home. My cat Boris helps fill the 'empty nest' syndrome that I sometimes get and I often feel guilty about spoiling him more than I did my children. But then again, because he's like an only child there's no one to complain that he gets preferential treatment. Boris is my constant companion and it's so nice not to feel that I live alone.

Demanding Kiki
Helen, 32

My oriental cat Kiki loves attention and would demand it every second of the day if I didn't go out to work. She follows me around all the time during the day at the weekend. Whatever I'm doing she has her face stuck in it. She'll even stand in an empty room calling for me to go to her. I go to where she is and pick her up, and she starts purring and butting me with her head. When I hear her shouting, I laugh because I know exactly what she wants.

She also flings herself down on the floor when you're walking across a room so that you can't avoid her. She wakes me up in the middle of the night by licking my face. We seem to have formed a very strong bond; I have heard that oriental cats are often like that. When I get home from work she's always waiting for me behind the door and I get a mew before she heads for the kitchen to show me that she needs feeding.

Kiki is very good at getting what she wants. She will just shout at you until you pay attention. It's impossible to do anything when she's demanding something from you. She loves to sit like a human on the sofa, upright and watching TV. She's also obsessed with pens. If I try to write anything she turns up and makes a grab for the pen. She will walk across the computer keyboard if I'm typing as well.

My story makes her sound like a nuisance but I love her to bits.

ME AND MY CAT

Feline Love
Chris, 32

We have recently acquired two kittens, never having had cats before. My girlfriend told her friend that we would take them and then talked me into it. They are gorgeous little creatures, always scampering about and playing funny games. I do like having them in the house very much. In a way though, I think they are little con artists – my girlfriend is convinced that they really love us, but I've noticed that they are only truly affectionate when they want a meal. Then afterwards it is back to their fun and games. But they are so cute, I can't really hold it against them.

Afterword

Just as there are all sorts of people in the world, it seems that there are all sorts of cats too. There are greedy cats, crazy cats, loving cats and interactive cats. Some cats are aloof, some are cuddly, some are nervous or bad-tempered, while others are sweet-natured or bold.

When we share our homes with cats, they become a part of the story of our life, and that means that they are there in both happy times and sad times. Reading these stories, we have encountered many people in different situations as well as hearing about their cats. I hope that you have enjoyed reading their tales, either because they remind you of cats you have known, or just for the fascination of getting a glimpse into the stories of ordinary people and their extraordinary cats.